THE SWEET SPOT

Increase Longevity Through Innovative Understanding of Blood Chemistry Labs

DR JOHN R. NIETERS L.AC, DAOM, CFMP
WITH **KATHRYN BLACK** L.AC, CFMP

For more information or to request interviews with the authors, email TheSweetSpotLabs@gmail.com.

ISBN: 979-8-88759-678-5 - paperback

ISBN: 979-8-88759-679-2 - ebook

DISCLAIMER

The information presented is the author's opinion and does not constitute any health or medical advice. The content of this book is for informational purposes only and is not intended to diagnose, treat, cure, or prevent any condition or disease.

It is sold with the understanding that the author and publisher are not engaged in rendering medical, health, or any other kind of personal professional services in the book. The reader should consult his or her medical, health, or other competent professional before adopting any suggestion in this book or drawing inferences from it.

Please seek advice from your healthcare provider for your personal health concerns.

This book and the information contained within is for informational purposes only and was based upon the review by the authors of information that was available at the time the book was written. Medical research and information changes daily, therefore the information contained in this book may be subject to change.

The author and publisher specifically disclaim all responsibility for any liability, loss or risk, personal or otherwise, which is incurred as a consequence, directly or indirectly, of the use and application of any of the contents of this book.

Get Your Free Gift!

To get the best experience with this book, I've created this video of the Top 10 labs you should ask your doctor to check every year (in many states you can order these yourself… if needed).

We have found that our patients who follow this advice are empowered towards better health.

You can get your gift by visiting:
https://TheBalancingPoint.net/free-gift/

To my wonderful family who has always supported me throughout all my adventures. To my beautiful wife who is always there for me. To my wonderful, loving children.

And certainly, to my magnificent patients who have taught me so much!

Thank you!

When the internal Qi is righteous, external evils cannot invade.

Huang Di Nei Jing

72ⁿᵈ chapter of Su Wen

TABLE OF CONTENTS

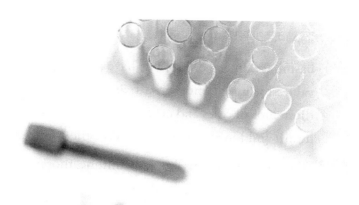

THE SWEET SPOT AND YOUR IDEAL HEALTHY BODY

We, the coauthors, wrote this book with the hope that it will assist in bringing excellent health to a great many people.

We wrote this book to inform people about the perfect healthy target range for laboratory values, so readers can better assess their health status and, if necessary, take early action if any of their laboratory values are outside the ideal healthy functional laboratory values.

When we write and use the term "laboratory values," what we're referring to are the levels of metabolic markers and the numbers and types of cells in a blood sample, such as the sample taken for routine testing for an annual physical.

In order for you to figure out where you stand when you receive your laboratory values, there are standards that have been set. The issue that we address in this book is that the "standards" that are still being used today were set a long time ago before many of these biological substances and the laboratory values for them were well understood.

A few decades ago, a few bright, enterprising medical doctors and PhDs got together and saw that the "standard" lab values they were basing treatment on did not have good proof that they were the ideal values for maintaining health and longevity. They set about studying thousands of cases and created databases to identify the ideal values for health and longevity (as opposed to the "standard" values).

What we do in this book is outline those ideal healthy functional values that, if maintained, will keep you in the "sweet spot" of the lowest likelihood of dying prematurely and of living the healthiest life possible for you.

We also give the actual studies that these ideal healthy functional values come from, and compare and contrast them to the "standard" values for given tests. You can use this information to better understand your lab values and take action (if necessary) to better your health, ideally on the front end before there's a major problem.

Let's look at the issue around "standard" laboratory values a bit further. When we look at individual tests, and compare the "standard range" of what is reported as "normal" with the ideal healthy functional values, we see that there are very large differences in statistical measures of mortality risk.

What this means is that you could have a value on a lab test that is within the so-called "normal range" and have as much as ten times the likelihood of dying over the next ten years as opposed to if your values were within the "sweet spot" range.

This can also explain how you can feel "not right" and go to your doctor, just to have them say that everything is normal. However, if they followed the "sweet spot" range, it may show where the actual problems are that make you feel that things are not quite right.

This book is a compilation of information referencing ideal healthy functional laboratory values. The information in this book is completely supported by valid peer-reviewed research studies from around the world. We also provide commentary on the studies that we feel are most valuable and accessible. We've also added a few stories from patients in our practice to support the importance of using healthy functional values.

It is important to remember, when all is said and done, none of this is "the truth." As new, updated research becomes available, the ideal values may change.

We wrote this book so that you can either read it from cover to cover, or you can look up the particular lab values that you are most interested in.

You can take your own laboratory tests and compare them with the values in this book to see if they are within the ideal functional ranges. If they are not within those functional ranges, you can look at the research studies cited in the book and the graphs indicating maximum health and see if it is necessary to make lifestyle changes in order to lower your mortality risk and better your health.

Because this verified research looking into ideal laboratory test values could add healthy years to most of the population of the world, we consider this book helpful to everyone. We think every adult should have a copy of this book.

This book can certainly empower you to help you take control of your health in a manner that you would never have thought possible before. This information can help you to open a dialogue with your (*hopefully* receptive) medical professional.

We are here if you need us.

To learn more about our us and our free educational website, go to www.TheBalancingPoint.net.

Again, keep in mind that the "standard" reference ranges do have great value in identifying acute and potentially serious chronic illness. However, they simply are not designed to lead us to maximum health and wellness.

Hopefully, as patients share this information, which is completely supported by quality research studies, it will inspire their medical professionals to move more toward a paradigm of creating long-term health and wellness.

Our Expertise

We, Dr. John R. Nieters and Kathryn Black, are the coauthors of this book. Because the aim of this book is to empower all people to better understand their health status in order to attain greater wellness, we think it's important you know from the start about our medical expertise.

About Kathryn Black, LAc, MSc, CFMP—I'm a licensed acupuncturist with a Master of Science degree, and I'm certified in functional medicine. I currently work as an acupuncturist and patient care coordinator alongside fellow coauthor Dr. John Nieters at the Alameda Acupuncture Clinic in Alameda, California. I specialize in combining Chinese medicine with the usage and insights of functional medicine lab values. I also specialize in inflammatory bowel disease and other digestive ailments.

I am responsible for writing the backbone of the book and providing the basic information for each of the lab tests.

I will also add that I started out as a patient of Dr. John Nieters, flying from Arizona to Alameda, California, for treatment. Soon after, I moved to Oakland, California, and began school at the Academy of Chinese Culture and Health Science to study acupuncture and herbal medicine. The Academy of Chinese Culture and Health Sciences is the third oldest acupuncture school in the USA and is unique in how it is very directly culturally focused to the Chinese paradigm in its orientation to the medicine.

In case the term "functional medicine" is new to you, I'll tell you about it. Dr. John and I are both functional medicine practitioners. What that means is that, as is true for any functional medicine practitioner, we generally make suggestions to our patients about lifestyle, diet, supplements, herbs, and other factors in order to improve the health of our patients before resorting to stronger pharmaceutical-based treatments that often have many more side effects.

About Dr. John R. Nieters, LAc, DAOM, DNBAO, MSc, CFMP, NCCAOM—I earned certificates in gynecology from Zhejiang University, China, and integrative diabetes care from Xin Hua Hospital in Hongzhou, China. My contribution to this book was to read hundreds of research studies, analyze them, simplify the information for public consumption, and speak about the studies. I also brought my several decades of clinical experience to add to the academic information.

I began my studies in Chinese medicine with Master Y.C. Chiang in Berkeley, California, studying Tai Ji Chuan and Qi Gong as well as being introduced to herbal studies. I continued my martial arts and contemplative studies as a master apprentice trainer at the Cheng Hsin School of Internal Martial Arts and Ontological Studies with 1978 World Martial Arts Champion, Peter Ralston. I was given a full teaching license to teach the Cheng Hsin arts in 1992. I received my Master of Science degree from the Academy of Chinese Culture and Health Sciences, ACCHS. I began teaching at ACCHS in 1998.

Shortly after graduation from ACCHS, I finished advanced orthopedics training and received the title of Diplomate National Board of Acupuncture Orthopedics (DNBAO).

I received my doctorate in 2009 from Five Branches University in San Jose, California. My area of specialization was gynecological endocrinology. I also did doctoral work on breast health at Zhejiang University, China.

I had my world rocked in 1998 when I attended my first course that combined traditional Chinese medicine with the principles of functional medicine. In one weekend, my brilliant instructor, Jake Fratkin, completely changed my approach to medicine and began my love of combining two worlds that fit together perfectly—traditional Chinese medicine combined with functional medicine diagnostics.

More On Traditional Chinese Medicine

In the course of the book, we, authors, as acupuncturists and practitioners of East Asian medicine, will be speaking from a particular perspective. Although we used the term "East Asian medicine," in the prior sentence, we will more often be using the term "traditional Chinese medicine." There are many schools, branches, and sub-branches of the medicine that we generally associate with countries of East Asia. The particular orientations and schools that the writers of this book attended, and taught at, called their art "traditional Chinese medicine."

While the general principles of traditional Chinese medicine, older forms of Chinese medicine, Japanese acupuncture, Korean acupuncture, and Vietnamese acupuncture arise from the same basic principles and ideas, there are subtle differences in treatment modalities and diagnostics.

Unfortunately, practitioners of traditional Chinese medicine (TCM) in the USA obtain licensure as "acupuncturists." While acupuncture is certainly a very important part of TCM, it is only one of the five major aspects of diagnostics and treatment with traditional Chinese medicine. The major treatment modalities are:

- Acupuncture and moxibustion (applying heat to the acupuncture point location)

- Herbal medicine

- Tui Na or hands-on manipulation and massage

- Dietary and lifestyle consideration

- Qi Gong exercise and energetic work

While it is unknown how old these practices are, they can be traced back with great accuracy for about 2,500 years in China. Some of the practices date back even earlier in India.

The remarkable discovery of the mummified body of "Otzi the iceman" clearly stands out as a fascinating query. Otzi is the man who was discovered in the ice fields in the Alps, located on the border between Austria and Italy, and had been dead for over 5,000 years. When examined by specialists, it was found that Otzi had tattoos located on the energy meridians of acupuncture points and even specific tattoos on major acupuncture points. This allows us to infer that the energetic system was well known by many cultures long before the Chinese formalized the acupuncture system itself.

The fact that this is such an ancient art caused many people to dismiss TCM as being non-scientific, but this is very inaccurate. The term that would apply is "pre-scientific." The Chinese were actually using the concepts that we call the "scientific method" 2,000 years ago. They simply didn't have the term "science."

It is, however, important to realize that the Chinese did not make up this system. They discovered the already existing nervous system in the human body and how to affect that nervous system 2,000 years ago.

In the book, *The Genius of China* by Robert Temple,1 the chapter on Chinese medicine contains many examples of the advances in Chinese medicine that were made well before that of European medicine.

It is quite unfortunate that acupuncture and herbal medicine is so grossly misunderstood in the USA, as it has so much to offer at such a low cost. Modern acupuncture and herbal medicine have a strong scientific basis.

We hope that in reading this book when you come across our mentions of TCM practices, that you'll be curious, open-minded, and hopefully interested enough to visit a practitioner of TCM yourself.

Be well.

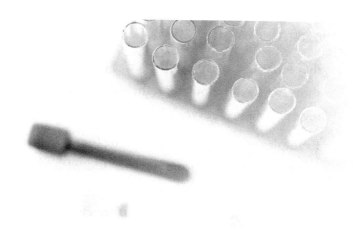

SOME CLARIFICATION TO HELP MAKE SENSE OF RESEARCH STUDIES DISCUSSED

You'll find in this book we frequently cite J-shaped and U-shaped curves in laboratory studies. Let's take a moment to explain their significance.

J-shaped and U-shaped curves are descriptions of data points forming distinct patterns. For our purpose of looking at laboratory values, both a U-shaped and a J-shaped curve will provide a "sweet spot."

The lowest point of the curve is the "sweet spot" representing the lowest risk of mortality, illness, or value we are investigating.

With the U-shaped curve, there is a relatively even distribution on both sides of the sweet spot indicating that higher or lower values can increase risk.

With a J-shaped curve, the arm to the left of the sweet spot will generally be shorter in length, indicating there are more values on the higher end of the curve. With the J-shaped distribution pattern, there will be more data points to the right of the sweet spot, which causes a curve that looks distinctly like the letter J lying on its side. Occasionally the short arm will be on the right side of the sweet spot. This is called a reverse J-shaped curve.

Examples of J-shaped curves can be found in several studies on alcohol consumption and mortality. Starting with the consumption of zero drinks per day and moving towards the consumption of one standard drink per day, we see a drop in mortality. As the number of drinks increases above the one standard drink per day, we see a steady increase in mortality risk.

The left side of the curve is very short from 0 to 1, whereas the right side of the curve is much longer and represents higher levels of alcohol consumption. So, we have a very short left arm to the left of the sweet spot, and a much longer arm on the right side of the sweet spot, forming a perfect J-shaped curve.

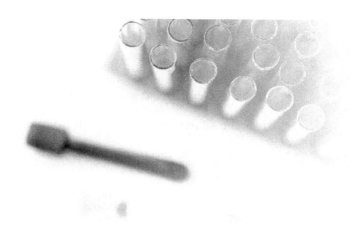

GLUCOSE

Major National Laboratory	65–99 mg/dL
Major HMO	60–99 mg/dL
Healthy Researched Values	82–89 mg/dL

AKA ...

- Blood sugar
- Blood glucose

FUN FACTS

- Glucose is from the Greek word γλυκύς (*glykys*), meaning "sweet."

- Glucose is also called dextrose.

- Glucose is one of a group of carbohydrates known as simple sugars (monosaccharides).

- It is found in fruits and honey.

- It is the major free sugar circulating in the blood.

- It is the source of energy in cell function.

- Blood glucose levels are regulated by insulin (a polypeptide hormone).

- The carbohydrates we eat are broken down into glucose (and a few other sugars), absorbed by the small intestine, and circulated throughout the body.

- Most of the body's cells prefer glucose for energy production.

- The brain and nervous system cells rely on glucose for energy and can only function when glucose levels in the blood remain within a certain range.

- The body's use of glucose depends on the availability of insulin, a hormone produced by the pancreas.

WHY GET TESTED?

- To determine if your blood glucose level is within the reference range.

- To screen for, diagnose, and monitor diabetes.

- To monitor blood glucose levels where required.

WHEN TO GET TESTED?

- It is recommended to have glucose levels checked during yearly blood work.

- If you have symptoms suggesting:

    o Hyperglycemia (high blood glucose)

    o Hypoglycemia (low blood glucose)

    o Pregnancy

    o Diabetes

WHAT IS BEING TESTED?

- Glucose is a sugar that serves as the main source of energy for the body.

- Insulin acts to control the transport of glucose into the body's cells to be used for energy.

    o It directs the liver to store excess glucose as glycogen (for short-term energy storage).

    o It promotes the synthesis of fats, which form the basis of a longer-term store of energy.

    o Balanced levels of glucose and insulin are essential for life.

- Normally, blood glucose levels rise slightly after a meal, and insulin is released to lower them.

    o The amount of insulin released matches the size and content of the meal.

- If blood glucose levels drop too low, such as in between meals or after a strenuous workout, then glucagon (another hormone from the pancreas) is produced to release liver glucose stores, thus raising the blood glucose levels.

- If the glucose/insulin system is working properly, the amount of glucose in the blood remains stable.

- Hyperglycemia and hypoglycemia, caused by a variety of conditions, can be life threatening. If severe and sudden changes in blood glucose levels occur, it could cause:

  o Organ failure, brain damage, coma, and—in extreme cases—death.

- Long-term high blood glucose levels can cause progressive damage to body organs such as the kidneys, eyes, blood vessels, heart, and nerves, such as occur in diabetes mellitus.

WHAT DO GLUCOSE RESULTS MEAN?

Glucose levels are increased by:

- Carbohydrate intake
- Stress
- Glandular and liver functions

Increased levels could be due to:

- Insulin resistance (insulin receptors not responding due to long-term hyperglycemia – high blood sugar)
- Acute stress response
- Diabetes
- High triglycerides (fats in the blood)
- Thiamine insufficiency (Vitamin B1)
- Defective production of insulin
- Decreased levels could be due to:
  - Fasting hypoglycemia

- Severe liver disease

- Hypothyroidism

FROM DR. JOHN

In measuring glucose levels in the blood, we are looking at how much sugar is in the bloodstream, in the serum. That's a critical thing to know. What is unfortunate is that the numbers, the values, and the manner in which the test is used are very poor indeed.

It is so poor that there was a recommendation made to major HMO and doctor groups over ten years ago saying not to use the glucose test as a diagnostic test for diabetes and pre-diabetes. They were instructed instead to use the hemoglobin A1c test.

The reason not to use the test as a marker for diabetes and pre-diabetes is that the serum glucose test is simply a spot check. It's saying, "At this instant in time, your blood sugar level is X."

There are many things that can affect that level on a spot-check basis. For example, a high stress morning or exercise can cause the release of blood glucose from the storage form of glucose, called glycogen, which will pump up the blood sugar temporarily.

I once had a patient that did as much as anyone that I have worked with to preserve and protect his health. He took the perfect supplements, ate an ideal diet, did yoga at 3 a.m., went for a long run before breakfast, and did intense work as a general contractor. He repeatedly had elevated fasting glucose, but we couldn't find any factors to account for this elevation. None of his labs could account for this imperfection.

Turns out, he lived very close to the testing lab and would go immediately after his run. When I had him change his routine for one lab test and not do any of these pre-testing activities, he came back with a normal blood sugar level. In the earlier tests, he was most likely releasing glucose from the glycogen store from his liver and muscle tissue.

Another potential and even more likely problem for elevated glucose levels in the blood would be dehydration. If there is less water per unit of volume of blood, then all the values in the lab report can be inaccurate. Since glucose is a fasting test, many people also neglect to drink fluids in the morning before getting their test done, which means the test will produce a higher-than-normal result for glucose levels.

A superior test for blood sugar pathologies is the hemoglobin A1c test. The hemoglobin A1c test is measuring the level of glycosylated hemoglobin. This test indicates the amount of blood sugar that the red blood cell has contacted during the three- to four-month lifespan of the red blood cells. This gives a much more accurate accounting of average blood sugar levels.

- Glycosylated—a sugar that is chemically bound to a protein

- Hemoglobin—the oxygen carrying molecules found on the red blood cells

- Red blood cells—the oxygen-carrying cells that circulate in the blood

    o Red blood cells have an average lifespan of 110 to 120 days.

- Glycosylated hemoglobin—the amount of glucose molecules that have become stuck to the hemoglobin molecules

When a hemoglobin A1c test is reported, it will also include an average value of the blood glucose for this three- to four-month period. This measurement of the amount of average blood sugar levels is a superb predictor of current and future cardiovascular, kidney, and eye pathologies that are directly related to high blood sugars.

An additional benefit of the hemoglobin A1c test is its ability to also note low levels of blood sugars. While low blood sugar levels are often overlooked, they can increase mortality just as much as high blood sugars can.

GLUCOSE, CARDIOVASCULAR, AND ALL-CAUSE MORTALITY RATE

In the study titled "Fasting Glucose and Its Association with 20-Year All Cause and Cause Specific Mortality in Chinese General Population,"[2] the conclusion was that "both low and high fasting glucose were significantly associated with increased risk of all-cause and cardiovascular mortality in Chinese general population." This indicates another classic J-shaped curve. You should note that there are similar studies showing similar results in the US population.

I like this study because of the way that they broke down the numbers, which I find to be very useful. They grouped results for the following glucose ranges:

- Under 60 mg/dL
- 60–69 mg/dL
- 70–79 mg/dL
- 80-89 mg/dL
- 90–99 mg/dL
- 100 – 109 mg/dL
- 110 – 125 mg/dL
- > 126 mg/dL

They used the range of 80–89 mg/dL as their reference group and compared that to the lowest group of under 60 mg/dL in terms of blood sugar levels. The under 60 mg/dL group had a 38 percent higher risk of death and a 2.58 times higher risk for cardiovascular disease.

That's an enormous difference. *Now, these are on the low side, meaning low levels of glucose in the blood, which is something doctors rarely comment on.*

Even if you get up into what are considered good ranges by a lot of doctors—let's say, 70–79 mg/dL—you're still going to see a 20 percent increase in all-cause mortality and about a 56 percent increase in cardiovascular disease. That increased risk of mortality and cardiovascular disease is seen with those having low blood sugar, albeit within a standard reference range by most labs.

In Dr. John's decades of working with patients and reading lab reports ordered by other medical providers, he has yet to have a patient report being counseled by their practitioner for glucose values in this 70–79 value range, with the exception of functional medicine providers.

As we can see, chronic low blood sugar is not as healthy as often perceived. Low blood sugar can be every bit as dangerous as chronic high blood sugar.

As an aside, these blood glucose levels, as well as several others of the values we will be examining are very consistent with the viewpoint of traditional Chinese medicine. One of the most common parameters and patterns that is looked for in pathologies is that of "deficiency" and "excess." In this study we see that "deficient" blood glucose and "excess" blood glucose are both significant risk factors.

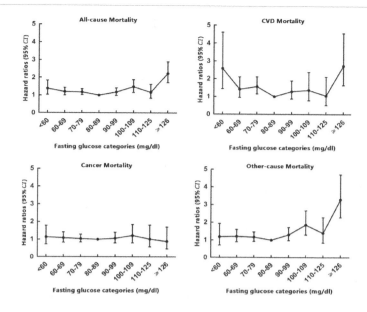

Figure 1: Multivariate-adjusted hazard ratios (95% CI) for all-cause and cause-specific mortality according to fasting glucose categories at baseline. Adjusted for age, sex, urbanization (urban or rural), region (north or south), types of work (mental, light manual, or heavy manual), education level (illiteracy, primary school, junior middle school, high school, or college), exercise habits (never, occasionally, or regularly), smoking status (current smoker or not), drinking status (current drinker or not), body mass index, systolic blood pressure, and serum total cholesterol at baseline.

LOW GLUCOSE AND CARDIOVASCULAR DISEASE

Another study that showed a classic J-shaped curve asked, "Is the current definition for diabetes relevant to mortality risk from all causes and cardiovascular and noncardiovascular disease?"[3]

The conclusion of this study was that "[t]he relation between mortality and glucose was J-shaped rather than showing threshold effect at high glucose levels." That means that high and low glucose are each markers of increased CVD (cardiovascular disease) and mortality. What we're looking at here are huge increases in death rate if the patient had either low or high blood glucose.

Another study, "Low Fasting Plasma Glucose Level As a Predictor of

Cardiovascular Disease and All-Cause Mortality,"[4] concluded that participants with low-fasting plasma glucose levels had a high risk of cardiovascular disease and all-cause mortality.

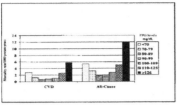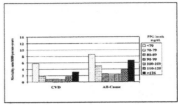

Figure 1. CVD and all-cause mortality rates per 1000 person-years, according to FPG levels. Rates in left panel are crude rates; rates in right panel are adjusted for age, sex, and population. FPG was classified as diabetes (≥126 mg/dL), impaired FPG (110 to 125 mg/dL), normal FPG (80 to 89, 90 to 99, and 100 to 109 mg/dL), and low FPG (70 to 79 mg/dL and <70 mg/dL). To convert values for glucose to millimoles per liter, divide by 18.01.

Figure 2: CVD and all-cause mortality rates per 1000 person-years, according to FPG levels. Rates in left panel are crude rates; rates in right panel are adjusted for age, sec, and population. FPG was classified as diabetes (≥ 126 mg/dL), impaired FPG (110 to 125 mg/dL), normal FPG (80 t9 89, 90 to 99 and 100 to 109 mg/dL), and low FPG (70 to 79 mg/dL and <70mg/dL). To convert values for glucose to millimoles per liter, divide by 18.01)

If the plasma glucose was under 70 mg/dL, there was a 3.3 times increased risk of cardiovascular disease mortality. ***That was an astronomical difference.***

Patients with a fasting plasma glucose of 70–79 mg/dL had over 1.5 times increased risk of death from cardiovascular disease.

That's pretty stunning for a value that is generally seen as being "normal"!

NEW "NORMALS" OF BLOOD GLUCOSE AND PRE-DIABETES

Another study titled "Creating a Pandemic of Pre-diabetes the Proposed New Diagnostic Criteria for Impaired Fasting Glycemia"[5] was not so much about identifying which ranges indicated the highest risk factors.

The researchers had already looked at these other studies and said, "Yes, obviously we're doing this wrong." They looked at creating new categories for diagnosing diabetes and pre-diabetes that would include the higher and lower levels that—up to that point—had been considered normal.

This was a study that was done in Denmark. Interestingly, the researchers found that by applying these new suggested values, the prevalence of impaired fasting glucose (diabetes and pre-diabetes) would go from 11.8 percent to 37.6 percent of the population.

Now, that's a little scary *or a lot scary*, depending on how you look at it. However, using the new tighter ranges could clarify when to start treatment for high or low blood sugars.

It's known that most patients have impaired fasting glucose levels for 10 years before they are accurately diagnosed. It is also known that most of the damage done by hyperglycemia is done within the first 10 years.

By changing from the currently used reference ranges to the new ranges proposed by these researchers, it may be possible to eliminate the majority of hyperglycemic damage.

In this way, we could move to preventing a problem rather than trying to repair damage. If you could discover that there was a diabetic risk 10 years earlier, you might prevent almost 100 percent of the damage.

RETHINKING HIGH GLUCOSE NUMBERS

Another study, "Normal Fasting, Plasma Glucose and Risk of Type Two Diabetes Diagnosis,"[6] looked at high-normal levels, up to 99 mg/dL.

Patients in this study with fasting glucose levels of 95–99 mg/L, which is within current normal ranges, were 2.33 times more likely to develop diabetes during the course of this study.

Subjects in the 90–94 mg/L group were 49 percent more likely to develop diabetes during the period of the study.

Longitudinal assessment (1992-2008) for progression to diabetes in 13,845 subjects (40-69 years old).

Supplementary Table 1. Life table of cumulative type 2 diabetes incidence by category of normal fasting plasma glucose

	Diabetes incidence according to categories of normal fasting plasma glucose		
	51-82 mg/dL	83-90 mg/dL	91-99 mg/dL
Years of follow up			
0	0.00%	0.00%	0.00%
3	0.08%	0.16%	0.50%
6	0.29%	0.32%	2.71%
9	0.59%	1.56%	6.82%
12	1.67%	4.56%	12.83%
15	3.54%	7.80%	25.86%

Figure 3: Longitudinal assessment (1992 – 2008) for progression to diabetes in 13, 845 subjects (40 – 60 years old). Life Table of cumulative type 2 diabetes incidence of category of normal fasting plasma glucose.

Supplementary Figure 1. Plot of cumulative type 2 diabetes incidence by category of normal fasting plasma glucose

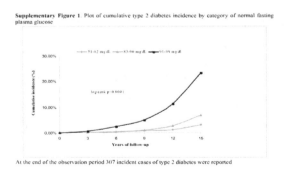

At the end of the observation period 307 incident cases of type 2 diabetes were reported

Figure 4: Plot of cumulative type 2 diabetes incidence by category of normal fasting plasma glucose. At the end of the observation period 307 incident cases of type 2 diabetes were reported.

To reiterate, all of the values shown in the above chart are inside the "normal range." What we are seeing in this chart is that subjects in the 90–94 mg/dL range were 49 percent more likely to progress to diabetes. This was done by a major health care system and looked at 46,578 members over a 10-year period.

This study has added importance based upon the large number of patients followed and the significant period of time during which they were followed. These are two very important factors to consider concerning the relevance of any research studies.

> **Comment by Dr. John**—I've had many patients come in with glucose measurements between 95 and 99 mg/dL, and their doctor had said to them, "Oh, you're great. Look at this—you don't have any glucose problems." I've also had them come in at 100–120 mg/dL, and their doctor said, "Well, we're going to keep an eye on it." As we can see from the study above, this would be bad advice.

GLUCOSE AND CARDIOVASCULAR RISK

Another study, "Fasting, Blood Glucose and Underestimated Risk Factor for Cardiovascular Death. Results from a 22-Year Follow-Up of Healthy Nondiabetic Men,"[7] indicated that the relative risk of death from cardiovascular disease for men with fasting blood glucose over 85 mg/dL was increased by 40 percent.

The conclusion was that fasting blood glucose values in the upper normal range appeared to be an important independent predictor of cardiovascular death in nondiabetic, apparently healthy, middle-aged men. Again, these fasting blood glucose values were well within the normal range, but on the higher end of the normal range.

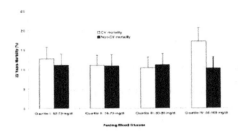

Figure 1—Crude 22 years cardiovascular and noncardiovascular mortality according to fasting glucose quartiles. Error bars indicate 95% CI. CV. cardiovascular.

Figure 5: Crude 22 years cardiovascular and noncardiovascular mortality according to fasting glucose quartiles. Error bars indicate 95% CI. CV. cardiovascular.

Another study that was very interesting, entitled "Increased Arterial Stiffness in Healthy Subjects with High-Normal Glucose Levels and in Subjects with Pre-diabetes,"[8] has a very strong J-shaped curve. Here, the researchers weren't looking at mortality as an end point. They were looking at arterial stiffness, which is a known precursor of cardiovascular disease.

The researchers were looking at levels of increased arterial stiffness in healthy subjects with high-normal glucose levels and in subjects with pre-diabetes. It indicated increased levels of arterial stiffness even within the current "normal ranges" of glucose. In conclusion, this study demonstrated that high blood glucose can be implicated in increased arterial stiffness.

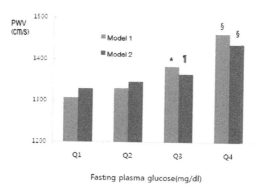

Figure 6: Mean values of brachial-ankle pulse wave velocity according to fasting plasma glucose quartile in non-diabetic healthy subjects. P<0.05 vs. Q1 and Q2, P<0.05 vs. Q1, Q2, and Q3, P<0.05 vs. Q1 Model 1; adjusted for age, sex. Model 2; adjusted for age, sex, systolic blood pressure, diastolic blood pressure, BMI, resting heart rate, Hs-CRP, HDL-cholesterol, and non HDL-cholesterol.

SUMMARY

- Blood glucose is looking at how much sugar is in the serum of the bloodstream.

- Blood glucose is a spot check. It's saying, "At this instant in time your blood sugar level is X."

- Fasting blood glucose levels higher than 88 mg/dL have been shown to be the beginning sign of many different diseases like diabetes and cardiovascular diseases.

- Fasting blood glucose lower than 82 mg/dL has been shown to be an indicator of the beginning of many different diseases, including cardiovascular disease and increased mortality risk.

- Therefore, we suggest a new "normal" for fasting glucose of 82–89 mg/dL.

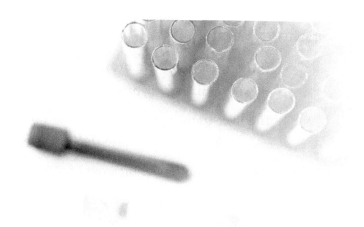

BUN

Major National Laboratory	5–18 mg/dL
Major HMO	7–27 mg/dL
Healthy Researched Values	12–19 mg/dL

AKA …

- BUN
- Blood urea nitrogen

FUN FACTS

- BUN is a waste product of protein metabolism.
- After we eat protein, the protein is broken down into several smaller compounds, including amino acids, that enter the bloodstream from the intestines to be used by cells throughout our body.

- This process of protein breakdown produces nitrogen-containing ammonia (as a byproduct).

- The liver transforms ammonia into urea to make it less toxic and sends the urea out into the bloodstream.

- The kidneys filter the urea out of the blood.

- If all is going well, there is a continuous amount of urea being produced and being excreted by the kidneys into the urine. The BUN level in the blood is, therefore, stable.

- If the kidneys are damaged and not functioning properly, urea and nitrogen are not properly filtered from the blood.

WHY TEST?

- Blood urea nitrogen (BUN) is a blood test performed as a marker of kidney function.

- It is also used to monitor the progression of kidney failure.

- It shows the difference between production and clearance of urea.

- Healthy kidneys take urea nitrogen out of your blood.

- When your kidneys are not working well, your BUN level goes up.

  o "BUNs get burned when you are dehydrated."

PURPOSE OF TEST

- **High or low levels can indicate a problem.**

  o Diseases that affect the kidneys or liver can change the amount of urea in the blood.

- o The liver may produce too much urea, or the kidneys may not be able to filter the waste out of the blood, which can cause levels to be high.

- **High levels may be seen due to any of the following:**
  - o Increased production or decreased excretion of BUN
  - o Gastrointestinal bleeding
  - o High protein diets
  - o Infection
  - o Dehydration

- **Low levels may be seen due to any of the following:**
  - o Liver failure
  - o Protein malnutrition
  - o Celiac disease
  - o Women who are pregnant
  - o Those who are overly hydrated

BUN AND MORTALITY

Journal of Insurance Medicine reported on a study entitled "Associations between Selected Laboratory Tests and All-Cause Mortality."[9] These researchers were very careful because this was about risk analysis, doing life insurance sales, and setting life insurance premiums.

The researchers found that the three most important findings for increased mortality in their studies were serum albumin, alkaline phosphatase, and BUN.

All of these tests were associated with mortality risks, even within the ranges that are generally considered clinically normal. It's important to remember that the healthy ranges that we are focused on in this book are often quite different from the "normal" or "reference" ranges that show up on a standard laboratory test.

The reference ranges are quite valuable to medical professionals in identifying acute, life-threatening conditions or serious chronic conditions. They should not, however, be relied upon as a measure of long-term good health and can be considered early warning signs of a trend towards health problems.

"Elevated Blood Urea Nitrogen Level as a Predictor of Mortality in Patients Admitted for Decompensated Heart Failure"[10] is an interesting study to look at the graphs and the curves. Importantly, it supports the tighter ranges of values that we are using for BUN, which is the ranges of 12–19 mg/dl.

"Commonly Used Clinical Chemistry Tests as Mortality Predictors"[11] reports the results from two large cohort studies. In these studies, 425,000 individuals were tested.

This particular study offers extremely useful U-shaped and J-shaped curves. These curves allow us to see the sweet spot where you are the healthiest. The sweet spot will literally be the lowest point on the data graph.

In a couple of the cases below, in terms of gamma-glutamyl transferase (GGT) and alkaline phosphatase, we see nearly linear graphs indicating that less is always better, and more is always worse.

For the other curves, we can see that there is a sweet spot (the very lowest spot in the curve) with elevations rising on both sides of the sweet spot to indicate increased mortality with higher or lower values than that found in the sweet spot.

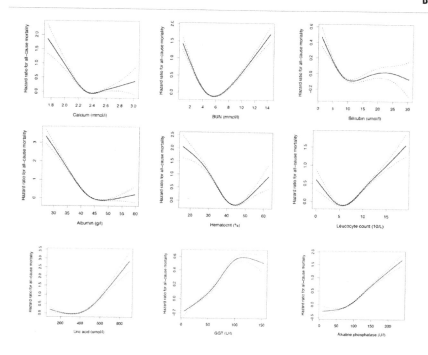

Figure 7: Relationships between nine clinical chemistry tests and all-cause mortality over nine years in the UK Biobank sample. The 10th percentile (dashed), median (solid) and 90th percentile (dashed) of the biomarkers are indicated by vertical lines. A restricted cubic spline function with three knots were used for the calculations with hazard ratio given as a solid line, upper and lower 95% confidence intervals as dashed lines

The study looked at a lot of different chemistry values. It looked at calcium, bilirubin, BUN (blood urea nitrogen), hematocrit, uric acid, and iron. For those tests, there was a U-shaped association.

For leukocyte count (white blood cells), gamma-glutamyl transferase (GGT), alkaline phosphatase, and lactate dehydrogenase, linear positive correlations were seen. This would show as either a straight line or a J-shaped curve.

To reiterate, a linear curve demonstrates that lower values are always better. This is similar to the linear graph we would see for cigarette smoking, where the lowest risk would be smoking zero cigarettes, smoking one cigarette would have a higher risk than no cigarette smoking, smoking two cigarettes would have a higher risk than smoking one cigarette, etc.

These are very interesting graphs that provide very useful information for computing a person's likelihood of living a long and healthy life.

SUMMARY

- BUN is a test to help us understand how well the kidneys are filtering.

- BUN levels above 19 mg/dL have shown an increase in cardio-vascular disease and mortality risk.

- BUN levels below 12 mg/dL have shown an increase in liver disease, malnutrition, and increased mortality risk.

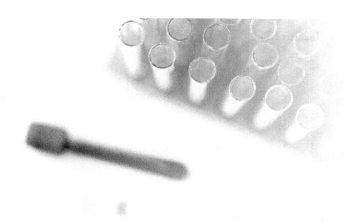

CREATININE

Major National Laboratory	0.76–1.27 mg/dL
Major HMO	< 1.11 mg/dL
Healthy Researched Values	0.9–1.3 mg/dL

FUN FACTS

- In 1886, Max Jaffe (1841–1911) identified the basic principles of how to identify creatinine and picric acid in an alkaline solution.[12]

- Creatinine is a chemical waste product in the blood. The blood passes through the kidneys to be filtered, and the creatinine is partially eliminated in the urine.

- Your body production of creatinine can vary based on a variety of factors.

- Creatinine will generally be excreted at a rate that will keep the serum levels fairly constant.

- The creatinine chemical waste is a byproduct of normal muscle function.

  o The more muscle a person has, the more creatinine they produce.

  o Levels of creatinine in the blood reflect both the amount of muscle a person has and their amount of kidney function.

- Factors that may affect the level of creatinine in the blood include body size, activity level, gender, and medications.

PURPOSE OF THE TEST

- Creatinine is a blood test that measures how well your kidneys work.

  o Clearing and filtering waste products out of your blood are important kidney functions.

INCREASED LEVELS

- Chronic renal dysfunction is the inability of the kidneys to accurately remove waste products and can cause creatinine levels to increase.

- Benign prostate hypertrophy, which refers to an enlarged non-cancerous prostate gland, can increase creatinine levels.

- Physical exercise can increase creatinine levels.

DECREASED LEVELS

- Serum creatinine is normally decreased in:

    o Children

    o Patients who have less-than-average muscle mass

    o Geriatric patients with reduced muscle mass

- Serum creatinine can be decreased in muscle-wasting disease.

LOOKING AT BOTH SIDES OF CREATININE

An article on creatinine with a fun title, "The Two Sides of Creatinine, Both as Bad as Each Other"[13] found that in acute and chronic kidney diseases (which are a very major public health problem), even very small rises in serum creatinine have been associated with increased mortality risk. This increased risk has been well appreciated in medical literature and practice.

In contrast, serum creatinine levels below normal range are far less appreciated in clinical practice and yet are equally important as high creatinine levels.

The conclusion of this study was that these researchers were quite concerned that low creatinine was not given enough credence.

These studies indicated in-hospital mortality of patients with a low serum creatinine, less than 50 micromoles per liter in the first 24 hours of admission, had higher levels of mortality.

This study is significant because it was done on over a million ICU patients from an ethnically diverse population.

The greater the number of participants in a study, the higher the likely validity of the study. (If we only have two participants in a study, we can't really draw much useful information from it.)

The ethnic diversity is significant as it helps to limit the effects of population-specific, genetic, and lifestyle orientations. This combination of ethnic diversity and the large number of subjects in the study creates a stronger likelihood of relevance to general populations.

SUMMARY

- Creatinine is primarily an indicator of creatinine clearance through the kidneys.

- Creatinine is a byproduct of creatine breakdown.

- Creatine is a component of muscle tissue.

- Creatine breakdown will be much higher after a significant exercise period.

- One thing to watch out for in this test is false elevated readings that are based upon intense workouts before the test is done.

- Low creatinine can also be an indication of danger just as is an increased creatinine level.

- Creatinine levels are the primary component that create the estimated glomerular filtration rate numbers (eGFR), which is the subject of the next chapter.

  o eGFR is derived from using a formula that combines several different factors. The most important of these being creatinine levels.

  o The glomeruli are the tiny filtering apparatus in the kidneys.

  o The filtration rate is an estimate of the effectiveness of the glomeruli in doing their job of filtering waste products so as to keep what the body needs and urinate out what the body needs to get rid of.

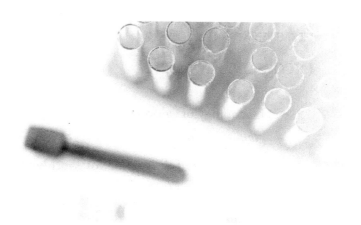

EGFR

Major National Laboratory	> 60 mL/min/1.73 m2
Major HMO	> 60 mL/min/1.73 m2
Healthy Researched Values	> 60 mL/min/1.73 m2

This is one of the few tests for which there are clear standard values. The issue isn't in the values themselves, but rather in the initiation of treatment for the different values.

In the case of estimated glomerular filtration rate, or eGFR, we're not going to speak about ideal ranges because the ranges have been well established and are tiered already.

AKA ...

- eGFR
- Estimated glomerular filtration rate

(NOT SO) FUN FACTS

- Etymology of "glomerular"—from the diminutive of the Latin *glomus*, meaning "ball of yarn" or "ball-shaped mass."

- Ten percent of the population worldwide is affected by chronic kidney disease (CKD).

- Millions die each year of chronic kidney disease because they do not have access to affordable treatment.[14]

- In people aged 65 through 74 worldwide, it is estimated that one in five men and one in four women have CKD.

- Two commonly used estimating equations for eGFR are:

   o CKD MDRD (modification of diet in renal disease).

   o CKD EPI (chronic kidney disease epidemiology collaboration) equations.

   o Using these equations, eGFR is calculated from the amount of creatinine in the blood.

- Race was originally included in eGFR calculations because clinical trials demonstrated that people who self-identify as Black/African American can have, on average, higher levels of creatinine in their blood.

   o It was thought this was due to differences in muscle mass, diet, and the way the kidneys eliminate creatinine.

   o Since a patient's race is not always used when laboratory tests are ordered, laboratories used different eGFR calculations for African American and non-African American people and included both numbers in their lab results.

WHAT IS BEING TESTED?

- The glomerular filtration rate (GFR) is a computed measure of your kidney function.

- Glomeruli are tiny filters in your kidney that allow waste products to be removed from the blood while preventing excess loss of important proteins and blood cells into the urine.

- The rate refers to the amount of blood that is filtered per minute.

- The main function of your kidneys is to clean your blood.

- Creatinine is one of the types of waste that the kidneys help to filter out of the body.

  o Therefore, if a high level of creatinine is found in your blood, it might signal that your kidneys (the glomeruli, in particular) aren't doing a good job of filtering and cleaning out your blood.

- An estimated glomerular filtration rate (eGFR) test is a blood test that's used to figure out how well your kidneys are doing their job.

  o The eGFR rate shows how much blood these glomeruli filter per minute, and it works by measuring the levels of creatinine in your blood.

  o The formula uses your creatinine levels, age, sex, weight, and race to arrive at that number—your eGFR.

MEASURING AND ESTIMATING GFR

- Getting an accurate GFR level is challenging.

o Measured GFR (mGFR) is a complicated and lengthy process, which is impractical for both clinicians and patients.

o It is for this reason that healthcare professionals use a formula to estimate GFR (eGFR).

- Reliable estimates of GFR are important for identifying kidney disease.

  o Often, there will be no symptoms of chronic kidney disease until just before the kidneys fail.

- The standard way to estimate GFR is with a simple blood test that measures your creatinine levels.

  o Creatinine is a waste product that comes from the digestion of dietary protein and the normal break-down of muscle tissue.

  o Aside from CKD, creatinine levels can be affected by other factors, including diet, muscle mass (the weight of your muscles), malnutrition, and other chronic illnesses.

WHY GET TESTED?

- You would get tested to determine the health and functionality of your kidneys.

- The eGFR is the easiest to understand and the simplest marker of kidney function.

KIDNEY DISEASE AND CARDIOVASCULAR DISEASE

Chronic kidney disease is considered present when the estimated glomerular filtration rate drops under 60. Below are the current tiers used:

- Stage 1—possibly some kidney damage with normal kidney function: eGFR < 90

- Stage 2—mild loss of kidney function: eGFR 89–60

- Stage 3A—mild to moderate loss of kidney function: eGFR 59–45

- Stage 3B—moderate to severe loss of kidney function: eGFR 44–30

- Stage 4—severe loss of kidney function: eGFR 29-15

- Stage 5—kidney failure: eGFR < 15

Let's look within those tiers at a few issues in terms of treatment in the study "The Link Between Chronic Kidney Disease and Cardiovascular Disease."[15]

It is well known that patients with chronic kidney disease (CKD) have strong risk factors for cardiovascular disease (CVD). The study is saying, however, that the excess risk of cardiovascular disease is only partially explained by the presence of traditional risk factors, such as hypertension and diabetes.

In the study's conclusions, while chronic kidney disease and cardiovascular disease share common traditional risk factors—such as smoking, obesity, hypertension, diabetes mellitus, and dyslipidemia—cardiovascular disease in chronic kidney disease patients still remains underdiagnosed and undertreated. The study points out the importance of clinicians recognizing that patients with kidney disease are a group at high risk for developing cardiovascular disease.

The association between chronic kidney disease and cardiovascular disease was first reported in 1836 by Dr. Bright, so this has been recognized for a considerable period of time. The impairment in renal function can increase the risk of cardiovascular disease two- to four-fold, possibly more.

One of the things pointed out in this study is that low eGFR combined with increased albumin is associated with a high incidence of cardiovascular disease, so they should be considered together.

In Stage 3 chronic kidney disease, there was a two-fold higher risk of cardiovascular disease. There was a three-fold higher risk in patients with Stage 4 chronic kidney disease when compared to patients with normal renal function.

FROM DR. JOHN

The eGFR is a very useful test that I call "Kidney Function for Dummies" because it's so simple to look at that one number and really get a good estimate over time of a patient's progress or lack of progress concerning kidney health.

A particular difficulty that I see in this area is that in my clinic (counting patients that have come to me with labs from other sources and labs that I've run), I'm estimating approximately 200 patients who have fallen into the category of Stage 3A chronic kidney disease (45–59 ml/min).

Only a small percentage of those patients were even informed that they had Stage 3A chronic kidney disease, and only a handful were given any meaningful suggestions about correcting the kidney condition.

I've found that the treatments that are generally used for Stage 4 kidney disease (15–29 ml/min), when started at Stage 3A kidney disease, can generally stop progression of the renal disease to worsening stages. In fact, if caught early enough, the renal damage as evidenced on the eGFR can often be reversed.

CASE STUDY 1—The first case study that I want to briefly mention is a 75-year-old Caucasian male with a history of diabetes mellitus type 2 who had two strokes that he has basically recovered from and who is now otherwise healthy. The patient presented to me four years ago with an eGFR of 53. In three months, we were able to move that from 53 to 74, with 53 being Stage 3 chronic kidney disease and 74 being much more normal and not a danger. After that, I did not see this patient for several years. He discontinued the treatment that I had suggested for him, and his eGFR dropped down to 44.

CASE STUDY 2—The second case study is the case of John Nieters who had four lithotripsies, a high-pressure pounding of the kidneys, for two very large kidney stones. After the four lithotripsies, his eGFR was down in the mid-40s. (Now remember, the eGFR can change slightly from day to day, so I am going to say the mid-40s.) Within six months of treatment, he had an eGFR up into the high 60s. Therefore, this chronic kidney deficiency condition is often reversible, but only if it is seen as reversible and treated at an early stage. Once it gets into Stage 2, chronic kidney disease is generally not reversible.

SUMMARY

- The eGFR test is one of the few laboratory tests for which there are clear standard values. The issue isn't in the values themselves, but rather in the initiation of treatment for the different values.

- Stage 3A chronic kidney disease is considered present when the estimated glomerular filtration rate drops under 60.

- Stage 3B chronic kidney disease is diagnosed when the eGFR is between 30 and 45.

- We've found that treatments generally used for Stage 4 kidney disease (when started at Stage 3A kidney disease) can generally stop progression of the renal disease to worsening stages.

  o This improvement can often be achieved when the renal deficiency is caused by metabolic disorders such as diabetes and high blood pressure, so long as the diabetes and high blood pressure are being effectively treated.

  o This would not be reversible in cases of true kidney disease, such as cancer, traumatic damage, or autoimmune dysfunctions.

- If caught early enough, the renal damage as evidenced on the eGFR can often be reversed.

URIC ACID

Major National Laboratory	2.5–7.1 mg/dL
Major HMO	2.5–7.5 mg/dL
Healthy Researched Values	Men: 3.7–5.3 mg/dL Women: 3.2–4.4 mg/dL

AKA ...

- Serum urate
- Uric acid

FUN FACTS

- If you ate too much on Thanksgiving, uric acid just might be the cause of the pain in your feet.

- Etymology of "uric" (adj.)—from the 1797 French word *urique*, "from urine," meaning "pertaining to or obtained from urine."

- In 1776, Swedish chemist Carl Wilhelm Scheele discovered uric acid in human urine and kidney stones. The same year, his discovery was confirmed by his colleague Torbern B. Bergman.[16]

- Uric acid is also found in the feces of birds, reptiles, and some mammals.

- Uric acid is notorious for the excruciating pain it produces in gout patients. When the acid is present in high concentrations in the blood, its low solubility causes it to solidify into sharp crystals in and around joints, notably in the feet.

- Uric acid concentration increases in the body when people consume large amounts of purine-rich foods such as red meat and seafood.

WHAT IS URIC ACID?

- Uric acid is a waste metabolite produced from the breakdown of purines.

  o Metabolite is a product of the breakdown of chemicals and other substances.

  o Purines are one of two chemicals used to make the building blocks of DNA and RNA.

- Uric acid is a purine metabolite that has numerous harmful physiologic effects, including:

  o Vascular smooth muscle cell proliferation (excessive growth of smooth muscle cells in the blood vessel system)

- Inhibition of nitric oxide production. (Nitric oxide is important for the health and effectiveness of the blood vessels.)
- Endothelial dysfunction (pathological changes in the cells lining the blood vessels)
- Oxidative stress (precursor to an inflammatory response)[17]

- The coronary system (heart) has shown to be a major site of production of urates, especially in the microvascular endothelium (lining of the small blood vessel).
- There is generally a net release of urate from the muscular tissue of the heart.

SOME CAUSES OF HIGH URIC ACID

- Diet high in purines:
  - Red meat
  - Organ meat
  - Seafood
  - High fructose corn syrup
- Obesity
- Dehydration
- Fasting
- Ketogenic diet
- Rapid weight loss
- Alcohol (Beer seems to be the worst.)
- Vitamin D deficiency

- Kidney disease

- Thyroid and parathyroid disorders

- Lead poisoning

- Genetic disorders

- Medications (water pills, chronic use of low-dose aspirin, niacin, immunosuppressants, chemotherapy, Viagra, testosterone)

- Lack of estrogen

- Aging

WHAT DOES IT MEAN?

- An excess of uric acid in the body is known as hyperuricemia.
  - o This can occur either when the body is producing too much uric acid or when the kidneys are not capable of eliminating it efficiently.
- A buildup of uric acid can cause problems in the long run, such as:
  - o Increased oxidative stress
  - o Inflammation
  - o Interference with normal tissue function (joints, kidneys)
- Elevated serum uric acid levels are associated with:
  - o Higher risk of hypertension
  - o Cardiovascular disease and mortality
  - o Progression of chronic kidney disease (CKD)

FROM DR. JOHN

We've decided to include uric acid in this book because, although it is not in a standard chemistry or metabolic panel, it is extremely important and even critical as a marker of long-term health and mortality. This is another test where the accepted reference ranges are inadequate for ensuring long-term health and reducing long-term mortality.

REVISING "NORMAL RANGES" FOR URIC ACID

In the study "Is It Time to Revise the Normal Range of Serum Uric Acid Levels?"[18] the researchers indicate that high uric acid may be more dangerous than previously thought.

There's a growing body of evidence that indicates that silent deposition of monosodium urate crystals (as would be found in gout and gouty arthritis) which would be indicated by a high uric acid level, may occur and lead to early destructive skeletal changes.

To quote from the aforementioned study, "In addition, a growing body of evidence demonstrates that uric acid might play a pathophysiological role." To explain this:

- "Patho-" is the prefix for pathologies or disease.
- "Physiological" means the way in which a body part functions.
- Hence, "pathophysiological" refers to the functional changes that accompany a particular disease.

The researchers also indicate additional dangers of high uric acid levels. These additional dangers seem to occur even without the deposition of monosodium urate crystals into the tissues.

They recommend that because of these findings, the healthy levels for uric acid should be reviewed and revised.

URIC ACID AND RENAL DISEASE

In the study "Uric Acid—A Uremic Toxin,"[19] the researchers point out that uric acid was often regarded as a simple marker of renal disease.

In this study, the researchers clearly hypothesized, and seem to prove, that uric acid at high levels causes renal disease and is not simply a marker for renal disease. They studied mild hyperuricemia without intrarenal (in the kidney) cysts and discovered that it increased:

- Systemic hypertension (high blood pressure)
- Glomerular hypertension (hypertension specifically in the glomeruli of the kidney)
- Afferent arterial sclerosis (narrowing of the arteries)
- Macrophage (white blood cells) infiltration in a normal rat kidney

They concluded that uric acid is not just a simple marker for, but also is causal for renal disease.

"Uric Acid, The Unknown Uremic Toxin"[20] is a review that brings together the concepts of uric acid metabolism and the method by which it affects the renal cells and renal function. The study also examined current therapies used to reduce hyperuricemia (or high uric acid) and avoid renal disease progression.

High uric acid plays an important role in many chronic diseases, including kidney diseases, gout, and pre-eclampsia in pregnant women.

There are several clinical trials in progress that show that hyperuricemia can be reduced to very low levels, which results in an increased glomerular filtration rate or more effective kidney function.

The study indicated that a reduction in high blood pressure could be achieved by lowering uric acid levels. The study also indicated that hyperuricemia could play a role in diabetic nephropathy (damage to the kidneys). Each of these studies is pointing to lower and lower levels of what is considered a normal range of uric acid.

In looking at many things in life, it can be very easy to confuse cause and effect when two things occur simultaneously. It has been assumed that diabetes and diabetic neuropathy caused high uric acid levels.

In this study we are seeing that the inverse can also be accurate, that high uric acid may also contribute to diabetic-related kidney disease. It may well be a two-way street, where either of these two conditions can contribute to causing the other condition.

RENAL DISEASE AND CARDIOVASCULAR DISEASE

While the study "Hyperuricemia and Long-term Outcome After Hospital Discharge and Acute Heart Failure Patients"[21] is moving somewhat away from the purpose of the book—to help otherwise normally healthy patients become aware of testing that may show the need for lifestyle, dietary, and other changes.

However, we mention the study because of some of the really wonderful information that it indicates.

The study looked at a mean uric acid level of 7.4 mg/dL, which is within most "normal" reference ranges for uric acid.

They found that there was an increased rate of death when compared to a uric acid level represented by the lowest quartile of this study. The rate of death at the level of 7.4 mg/dL, was approximately double the rate of death of the patients with a uric acid level of under 5.8 mg/dL.

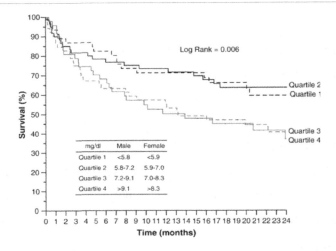

Figure 8: Kaplan-Meier curves showing cumulative survival free from the composite endpoint of all-cause death and/or new HF hospitalization, according to the UA quartile (adjusted for sex).

This increase in mortality continued for several years after the initial testing was done, and it indicated that hyperuricemia remains an independent risk factor for adverse outcomes in patients and patients with heart failure or other cardiac problems for at least 24 months. This would seem to indicate that patients with even slightly elevated uric acid had a higher mortality risk without any other cofactors being involved.

The study "Serum Uric Acid Shows a J-shaped Trend with Coronary Mortality in Non-insulin-dependent Diabetic Elderly People"[22] clearly indicated that low uric acid levels also increased mortality risk by approximately 34 percent.

- For the first tertile:

    o Uric acid levels were less than 5.22 mg/dL.

    o The death rate was 7.9 percent.

    o Death was 34 percent higher in the first tertial than the second tertial.

- For the second tertile:

    o Uric acid levels were between 5.4–6.48 mg/dL.

    o The death rate was 5.9 percent.

    o This tertile was used as the reference range.

- For the third tertile:

    o Uric acid levels were above 6.66 mg/dL.

    o The death rate was 12.1 percent.

    o The death rate in this tertial was more than double the death rate in the reference range.

SUMMARY

- Uric acid is a waste metabolite produced from the breakdown of purines.

- A buildup of uric acid can cause problems such as:

    o Increased oxidative stress

    o Inflammation

    o Interference with normal tissue function (joints, kidneys)

- Elevated serum uric acid levels are associated with the following:

    o Higher risk of hypertension

    o Cardiovascular disease and mortality

    o Progression of chronic kidney disease (CKD)

- Patients with low serum uric acid levels have increased cardio-vascular risk.

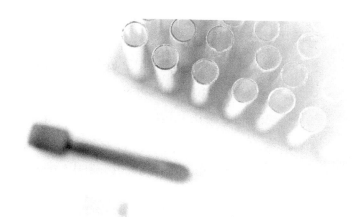

SODIUM

Major National Laboratory	134–144 mmol/L
Major HMO	135–145 mEq/L
Healthy Researched Values	139–142 mmol/L

FUN FACTS

- Sodium bears the atomic number 11 in the periodic table with the symbol Na+.

  o "Do you know any sodium jokes? Na."

- Our word "salary" derives from "*salarium*," which is a term for salt given to Roman soldiers as part of their wages.

- Sodium was first isolated in 1807 by Humphrey Davy.

- As it is a very reactive molecule, sodium is never found by itself without association to other compounds.

- Its symbol and name derive from the Latin "*natrium*" or

"*arabic natrun*" and the Egyptian word "*ntry*" (natrun), all of which refer to soda or sodium carbonate.

- It is the sixth most abundant element on Earth.

- Sodium comprises 2.6 percent of the Earth's crust—making it the most abundant alkali metal (strong bases capable of neutralizing acids).

- Sodium is the most common dissolved element, along with chloride, in the oceans (as measured by weight).

- Sodium is highly water soluble.

- Sodium is what gives fireworks their gold or yellow color.

FUNCTIONS OF SODIUM

- It is an essential element in the body.

- It is both an electrolyte and mineral.

- Most of the sodium in the body (about 85 percent) is found in blood and lymph fluid.

- The amount of sodium in plasma is controlled by the kidneys under the influence of the hormone aldosterone, which is secreted by the adrenal gland.

- If dietary sodium exceeds requirements, the excess is excreted by the kidneys.

- Sodium is essential to cellular function for many reasons, for example:

  o Maintenance of fluid balance in the cells and the extracellular fluids

  o Absorption of nutrients such as glucose

  o Critical to the function of the human nervous system

to conduct nerve impulses

- ○ Needed for muscles to contract and relax

- ○ Key role in the control of blood pressure

- Sodium creates specific channels in our cell membranes, which carry out different vital tasks.

  - ○ A channel can be classified based on what will trigger it to open.

  - ○ This can be either a "voltage-sensitive" channel or a "binding of a substance" channel.

  - ○ The sodium-potassium pump's purpose is to:

    - Pump three sodium ions out of a cell and two potassium ions into it.

    - You can think of a banana floating in the ocean. The cell inside (banana boat) prefers potassium inside while the cell outside (ocean) prefers more sodium/salt.

  - ○ The sodium-potassium pump is important for nerve cell function, as it supports nerve cells in maintaining the resting potential of a neuron.

  - ○ Swelling of a cell can occur when the sodium-potassium pump doesn't function properly.

- These channels support the following:

  - ○ They control the amount of water that gets into and out of cells.

  - ○ They allow the transport of specific nutrients and compounds into cells, for example: amino acids, glucose, vitamins.

o   They assist the muscles and heart in contracting.

o   They allow nerve cells to carry messages (nerve impulses) between the brain and body.

FROM DR. JOHN

Sodium is one of my absolute favorite topics to talk about with patients. The reason is that there is so much good, solid, scientifically proven information about the importance of maintaining very narrow ranges of serum sodium, yet medical doctors rarely speak about it unless patients have grossly elevated sodium levels (hypernatremia) or grossly low sodium levels (hyponatremia). The topic regarding sodium tends to most frequently occur in conversations regarding blood pressure and minimizing salt intake.

The reality is that there are dozens upon dozens of very well-done research papers showing that there's a clear U-shaped curve for sodium. If you get too low, there's a much greater chance of:

- Death from stroke

- Higher rate of injury or death due to falling

- Higher rate of bone fractures

- Higher rate of certain types of strokes

- Certain types of cancers

And this isn't a standard reference range low you would find on a blood chemistry test.

Yes, if it's low in the range that you would see on one of the lab commercial companies, it's certainly going to be out of range. If you're too low on the narrower functional ranges, it is also a problem.

On the other hand, high sodium is extremely dangerous.

It increases risk for:

- High blood pressure
- Heart attack
- The blood becoming thicker and harder to pump

And so those ranges that we see on what's called a "standard range" or a "reference range" are unfortunately not very accurate for maintaining health. When we look at the U-shaped curve that shows 138–140 mmol/L, maybe pushing up to 141 mmol/L is the sweet spot (at the very bottom of the U-Shaped curve where people's sodium level should be for best health). And the real ideal sweet spot is 139–140 mmol/L.

When you get under 137 mmol/L, you start seeing more adverse events, and when you get over 142 mmol/L, you start seeing more adverse events. It's shockingly apparent that there are huge differences in mortality with those tiny changes in sodium range.

Only once a month or less, do I have a patient come in with a lab test we ordered, or a lab from somewhere else, with a high sodium level. It's just not common.

We have become a culture that is very salt-intake conscious, which is generally a good thing.

Because of a rampant epidemic of adrenal problems, I see far more low sodium levels every week and sometimes daily. I see low sodium levels, and patients are often having symptoms from those low sodium levels. Symptoms of low sodium are:

- Orthostatic hypotension, which is dizziness when you stand up.
- Sometimes nausea
- A sense of cognitive problems

CASE STUDY—PATIENT WITH LOW SODIUM

A delightful, female patient came in and was really, really upset—upset as in anxious. She had an A-type personality—a very fast-paced, rapid-speaking, and hard-charging person.

She was practically in tears as she said to me, "Dr. John, I've been to several doctors and alternative doctors, and nobody can help me. Every day when I get up to drive my daughter to school, I get sick, I get nauseous, I get lightheaded, I get motion sickness. I have to pull the car over and sit there for quite a while until I can regain my senses and continue to drive her to school."

I asked a couple of what I thought were very logical questions. One was: "How long has this been occurring?" She said only a couple of months. She'd never had problems with it before.

I said, "I'm sitting here with your blood test, and the first thing that I see is that your sodium levels are low, from a functional standpoint. And also, your potassium levels are off. But I'm more concerned about the sodium right now."

Then I asked a second question, "What do you do before you drive your daughter to school?"

She said, "I get on my Peloton bike, and I ride."

I then asked, "So, do you take a casual ride?"

She said, "No, I'm driven. I get on for an hour, and I go as hard and as fast as I can. I'm very competitive."

I asked, "Do you perspire much?"

She said, "Yeah, I have to put towels down around the bike because I perspire so much."

I said, "Okay, I have a fix for your problem. I think it's going to be really expensive [I was joking], but I think we can fix it. I want you to do half a teaspoon of salt about an hour before you get on your Peloton. And I want you to sip electrolytes and salt all through the day."

She came back in three weeks. All of her problems were gone. No problems whatsoever. And they haven't returned. Now, since then, she's agreed to not exercise quite as intensely. But the problem, the entire issue, was low sodium.

SALT PHOBIA

Now the next issue is, we as a culture have become very salt phobic. Salt is a generic term, but here we're using it to mean sodium chloride, which is common table salt. There are a few other minerals if you get good quality salt.

The recommended dietary sodium intake is far lower than the natural intake that humans have used throughout our history. And this can be determined by teeth samples, etc. So, the current most common practice recommends sodium levels that may be actually functionally too low.

Some people are sodium sensitive and need to be careful about their sodium intake. However, Dr. John finds his more clinically ill patients are more sensitive to low sodium levels.

We are certainly not recommending that everyone fills up their salt shakers. We're merely pointing out that one size does not fit all.

SALT AND ADRENALS

Most of Dr. John's patients are chronically ill and middle aged or older. Most have had very intense lifestyles. They're kind of worn-out in a lot of ways and are what would commonly now be called "in a state of adrenal fatigue." We know and talk about a lot of the adrenal hormones—cortisol, epinephrine, and norepinephrine. The general public now has a pretty good idea about what those do.

However, one of the key adrenal hormones is aldosterone. Aldosterone is a primary controller of sodium-to-potassium ratios. If you have an increase in intake of sodium, your aldosterone and other hormones are working properly, and your kidneys are working properly, then you'll just pee out the excess sodium.

The same is true with potassium because the body is trying to keep you in a state of homeostasis. If the kidneys are out of balance, or if your aldosterone levels are too high or too low, you won't have a proper sodium-to-potassium balance.

SODIUM, ALDOSTERONE, AND HYPOVOLEMIA

Most of Dr. John's patients who have burned the candle at both ends for many, many years have low aldosterone. Aldosterone is produced at the very outer layer of the adrenal glands. And in many of his patients, it's LOW.

Low aldosterone is directly related to low sodium. And the low sodium will cause less blood volume because it doesn't attract water into the serum. With this, you literally have hypovolemia:

- "Hypo" means low or lower.
- "Volemia" pertains to low volume, in this case of blood or fluids.

In this case we are speaking of mild hypovolemia. Severe hypovolemia can cause shock and even death. Symptoms of mild hypovolemia include dizziness, fatigue, weakness, and lightheadedness.

Hypovolemia is very difficult to test for from a Western standpoint.

When you look at blood values, say, on the CBC (complete blood count), you look at your red blood cells, white blood cells, and hemoglobin, etc. Those are all values per unit of blood volume, so they don't truly reflect absolute values.

We can't really test for blood volume without using some mechanism to actually measure the amount of fluid in your bloodstream (which is not very practical in a clinical setting). They would have to take all your blood out, measure it, then put it back in.

And that's the advantage we have with traditional Chinese medicine. When we feel a patient's pulse at the radial arteries on the wrists, we can feel hypovolemia. We can feel low blood volume as the arteries have a very different feeling under pressure. And when we feel a hypovolemia pulse, we ask patients if they get dizzy when they stand up. The response: over 90 percent of the time they say yes. We follow that up with a couple of in-office tests of adrenal function, and they generally confirm our diagnosis.

The point is that you can have low sodium intake, or you could have normal sodium intake and low aldosterone levels, and either way, you'll have low serum sodium. There are other possible causes for having low sodium, but those are the two most common causes that we see.

Our recommendation is that if you ever test low for sodium, or even more importantly, if the sodium-to-potassium ratio is off, you should get your blood chemistry done three to four times a year to make sure you have not fallen back into a state of low sodium. This is an extremely inexpensive test.

Technically, the term "hyponatremia" is used to describe low sodium. When we mention hyponatremia in the following studies, you'll know what I'm talking about.

SODIUM AND BONE HEALTH

We start by looking at "Hyponatremia, Falls and Bone Fractures. A Systematic Review and Meta-Analysis."[23]

A meta-analysis is generally one of the best forms of research because you're taking a lot of individual studies and putting them together. Sometimes that's a little difficult to do. Sometimes you're comparing apples to oranges. However, when your numbers are higher and you have more participants and studies to evaluate, the research is more likely to be valid.

This study supports low sodium levels as being a factor in falls and in bone fractures. A fairly large number of older patients fall from hyponatremia and orthostatic hypotension (where they get dizzy upon standing).

When they get up in the middle of the night to go to the bathroom (which most older people do several times a night), they get up, get dizzy, fall down, and fracture bones. Once you go into the hospital with a fractured hip, your odds of leaving alive are very low. In addition, many of these people fall and will actually get skull fractures or brain bleeds and die, so this is a very serious issue.

In a Rotterdam study, "Mild Hyponatremia as a Risk Factor for Fractures,"[24] the key word is "*mild.*" They tracked 5,208 elderly subjects. They looked at a definition of hyponatremia as sodium levels of less than 136 millimoles per liter. That is a level that is higher than some of the lower cut-off points on certain labs.

They found the following:

- Increased risk of vertebral fractures (spinal fractures) was 78 percent higher.

  o This means that there was almost double the risk of falling and fracturing of the bones if their sodium level was under 136 mmol/L.

- Also, all-cause mortality was higher in subjects with hyponatremia.

  o They died at about a 20 percent higher rate during the course of the study.

So, again, we're looking at some really severe consequences.

When we add the increased risk of hyponatremia in the elderly to an already increased risk of falling because of balance issues and pain issues. In addition, there is often the over prescription of blood pressure medications with the elderly.

I've seen many elderly patients who were put on blood pressure medications. Their blood pressure came down into a normal range or even became low, and they were never taken off the medications. That combination of low sodium, being elderly, reduced balance, and blood pressure medications can be very deadly. I'm quite clear about this as it is the combination of factors that killed my own mother.

Now, don't increase your salt intake without talking to your practitioner, and certainly do not change your blood pressure medications without speaking with your medical doctor.

My point is that your ***sodium should be checked frequently***, or your elderly parents' sodium should be checked frequently. Their ***blood pressure should be checked frequently*** to make sure that the dosage of blood pressure medication is still correct.

SODIUM AND STROKE

There is a study called "Hyponatremia in the Prognosis of Acute Ischemic Stroke"[25] and in its conclusion, there is a higher mortality rate in these patients with hyponatremia. This was shown even after they had a stroke and were tracked for 12 months post stroke. They still maintained a higher possibility of an additional stroke during this 12-month period, and mortality was significantly higher.

- "Ischemia" means a lack of blood flow.

- A stroke is a cerebral vascular accident in the brain.

Let's look at another study called "Frequency of Electrolyte Imbalance in Patients Presenting with Acute Stroke."[26]

- "Ischemic stroke" means a brain accident from lack of blood flow.

- "Hemorrhagic stroke" means a brain accident from bleeding in the brain.

- "Acute" means sudden onset.

- "Electrolytes" are minerals that are carried in the blood, such as potassium, calcium, sodium, etc.

The outcome here was the following:

- The sodium level was significantly lower in the ischemic stroke group as compared to the hemorrhagic stroke group.

- The potassium level was significantly higher in the hemorrhagic stroke group compared to the ischemic stroke group.

In "Serum Sodium Concentration and Risk of Stroke in Middle-Aged Males,"[27] it was shown that "sodium concentration is related to the risk of stroke even at levels of sodium usually regarded as normal." This study was looking more at high sodium levels and the risk of stroke.

SODIUM AND ANEMIA

Something that's also very common in the elderly is anemia. There are some estimates of over 400 types of anemia, but here we're talking about the most commonly diagnosed, iron deficiency anemia.

In another similar study, "Evaluation of Serum Electrolyte Levels in Patients with Anemia,"[28] they found that:

- Sodium levels and potassium levels are impacted in patients with anemia.

- There should be closer monitoring of serum electrolyte levels in patients that have been diagnosed as anemic.

So once again, don't look at anemia without looking at electrolyte levels.

SODIUM AND CARDIOVASCULAR DISEASE

Another study, "Mild Hyponatremia, Hypernatremia and Incident Cardiovascular Disease and Mortality in Older Men, a Population Based Cohort Study,"[29] is one that might be really fun for you to pull up. Yes, those are a lot of big words, and it's a lot of information to look through, but they have the best U-shaped curves.

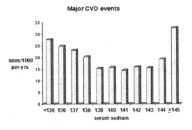

Figure 9 Serum sodium concentrations and incident cardiovascular rates/1000 person-years and total mortality rates/1000 person years. Number of men: Sodium levels <136 (n = 207), 136 (n = 134), 137 (n = 234), 138 (n = 330), 139 (n = 463), 140 (n = 494), 141 (n = 491), 142 (n = 337), 143 (n = 244), 144 (n = 109), ≥145 (n = 56).

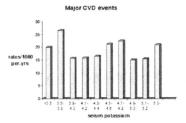

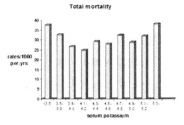

Figure 10: Serum potassium concentrations and incident cardiovascular rates/1000 person-years and total mortality rates/1000 person years. Number of men <3.5 (n = 12), 3.5–3.8 (n = 118), 3.9–4.0 (n = 341), 4.1–4.2 (n = 535), 4.3–4.4 (n = 664), 4.5–4.6 (n = 652), 4.7–4.8 (n = 209), 4.9–5.0 (n = 444), 5.1–5.2 (n = 68), ≥5.3 (n = 39).

The U-shaped curve, in this case, shows the following:

- The sweet spot for lowest mortality for serum sodium is 140 mmol/L.

- Under 139 mmol/L is where mortality starts to climb on the low end of the range.

- Over 141 mmol/L it starts to climb on the high end of the range.

- So, 140 mmol/L is absolutely the sweet spot.

Now, when it comes to cardiovascular events, it is found that sodium between 139 and 141 mmol/L is about the same. You get a slight increase in cardiovascular risk when sodium is 142 and 143 mmol/L.

When sodium drops below 139 mmol/L, the rate of increase in mortality is quite dramatic. In fact, between 136 and 139 mmol/L, the rate of cardiovascular events is very nearly double.

SODIUM AND MORTALITY

Another study, "Small Increases in Plasma Sodium Are Associated with Higher Risk of Mortality in a Healthy Population,"[30] has another beautiful U-shaped curve in it.

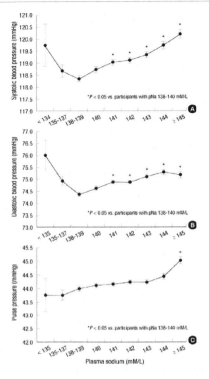

Figure 11: Distribution of systolic blood pressure (SBP), diastolic blood pressure (DBP), and pulse pressure (PP) according to plasma sodium (pNa) levels. (A) SBP according to pNa levels. SBP in participants with pNa ≥ 141 mM/L was significantly higher than in pNa 138-139 mM/L (P = 0.002), and SBP was not significantly different among participants with pNa < 134 and pNa 138-139 mM/L. The SBP is adjusted by age, estimated glomerular filtration rate, body mass index, total serum cholesterol, protein, calcium, phosphorus, glucose, potassium, HDL cholesterol, and alkaline phosphatase using covariance analysis (ANCOVA). Error bars indicate the standard error of the mean. (B) DBP according to pNa levels. DBP in participants with pNa ≥ 141 mM/L was significantly higher than in participants with pNa 138-139 mM/L (P < 0.001). The DBP is adjusted by age, estimated glomerular filtration rate, body mass index, total serum cholesterol, protein, calcium, phosphorus, glucose, potassium, HDL cholesterol, and alkaline phosphatase using covariance analysis (ANCOVA). Error bars indicate the standard error of the mean. (C) PP according to pNa levels. Only pulse pressure (PP) in pNa ≥ 145 mM/L participants was significantly higher than in pNa 138-189 mM/L participants. The PP is adjusted by age, estimated glomerular filtration rate, body mass index, total serum cholesterol, protein, calcium, phosphorus, glucose, potassium, HDL cholesterol, and alkaline phosphatase using covariance analysis (ANCOVA). Error bars indicate the standard error of the mean. `P < 0.05 vs participants with pNa 138-140 mM/L.

This study indicated that women 50 years of age and older showed a significant association between sodium and all-cause mortality. They go into a lot of research about the perfect levels of sodium that you need to have in your system. And, once again, we're looking in that

139–140 mmol/L range as the sweet spot.

SUMMARY

- Sodium is an important test marker that is often overlooked.

- Physical symptoms can be observed when sodium levels are slightly too high or too low.

- Sodium levels below 138 mmol/L show a greater chance of the following:

  o Death from stroke or falls

  o Higher rate of bone fractures

  o Higher rate of certain types of strokes

  o Certain types of cancers

  o Adrenal problems

  o Orthostatic hypotension, which is dizziness when you stand up

  o Nausea

  o A sense of cognitive problems

- Sodium levels above 141 mmol/L increase the risk for the following:

  o High blood pressure

  o Heart attack

  o The blood getting thicker and being harder to pump

  o Death from stroke.

POTASSIUM

Major National Laboratory	3.5–5.2 mmol/L
Major HMO	3.5–5.3 mEq/L
Healthy Researched Values	4.0–4.4 mmol/L

FUN FACTS

- Potassium has the periodic table symbol K (from Neo-Latin "*kalium*") and atomic number 19.

- It is indispensable for both plant and animal life.

- Potassium imparts a lavender color to a flame.

- It is the seventh most abundant element in Earth's crust, consisting of 2.6 percent of its mass.

- It is the third most abundant mineral in the body.

- Potassium was the first metal to be isolated by electrolysis by the English chemist Sir Humphrey Davy in 1807.

- o He obtained the element by decomposing molten potassium hydroxide (KOH) with a voltaic battery.
- It was first isolated from potash, the ashes of plants, from which its name derives.
- Potassium is a mineral that forms positive ions (electrically charged particles) in solution.
- It is an essential constituent of cellular fluids.
- The storage of potassium in body cells is dependent on maintenance of a proper ratio with calcium and sodium.
- Approximately eight percent of the potassium that the body takes in through food consumption is retained. The rest is readily excreted.

FUNCTIONS OF POTASSIUM

- Potassium, the principal intracellular cation (a positively charged ion), occurs in plasma at a much lower concentration than sodium.
- The renal excretion of potassium is influenced by aldosterone, an adrenal hormone which causes retention of sodium and loss of potassium.
- Potassium helps regulate fluid balance, muscle contractions, and nerve signals.
- Potassium is important for normal muscle and nerve responsiveness, heart rhythm, and intracellular fluid pressure and balance.
- The kidneys are centrally involved in regulating potassium levels, a potassium test can be used to help evaluate the status of your kidneys.

- Potassium also plays an important role in healthy heart function.

  o It is involved in the electrical signal of the heart muscle.

- Ninety-eight percent of potassium in the body is found inside the cells. Of this potassium:

  o Eighty percent is located in your muscle cells.

  o Twenty percent can be found in your bones, liver, and red blood cells.

- When potassium is inside your body, it functions as an electrolyte.

  o When in water, an electrolyte dissolves into positive or negative ions that could conduct electricity.

  o Potassium carries a positive charge.

  o Electricity in your body provides the processing of fluid balance, nerve signals, and muscle contractions.

LOW POTASSIUM COULD MEAN:

- Not enough potassium in diet
- Gastrointestinal disorders, chronic diarrhea, vomiting
- Use of diuretics (pills that promote urination)
- Excessive laxative use
- Excessive sweating
- Folic acid deficiency
- Certain medications such as corticosteroids and some antibiotics and antifungals
- An overdose of acetaminophen

- Diabetes, particularly after taking insulin

- Chronic kidney disease

- Hyperaldosteronism (when too much aldosterone hormone is released from adrenals)

- Cushing's syndrome (a disease of the adrenal glands)

HIGH POTASSIUM COULD MEAN:

- Having too much potassium in diet

- Taking potassium supplements

- Taking some medications, such as:

    o Nonsteroidal anti-inflammatory drugs (NSAIDs)

    o Blood pressure medications

        - Beta-blockers

        - ACE enzyme inhibitors

        - Angiotensin II receptor blockers

FROM DR. JOHN

One of the more often discussed and studied of the blood chemistry components is potassium because of its implication in a large number of potentially negative health conditions and its relationship to a mortality curve.

Much of the potassium research has been undertaken by observing adverse outcomes in patients that had chronic kidney disease, hospitalized patients, and patients with acute medical conditions. Very little of the research on potassium has been done while observing specific ranges in a relatively healthy population.

We will be looking at mortality in community living populations while observing the effects of high potassium, low potassium, and potassium even within what were formerly considered "normal ranges."

POTASSIUM AND CARDIOVASCULAR RISK

When investigating potassium levels, we recommend that you start with "The Relation of Syrian Potassium Concentration with Cardiovascular Events and Mortality in Community Living Individuals."[31] This is a good place to start if you have an interest in studying the effects and the mortality ratios concerning potassium levels. This study has well-done graphs and U-shaped curves, and it's the number one study for looking into optimal potassium values.

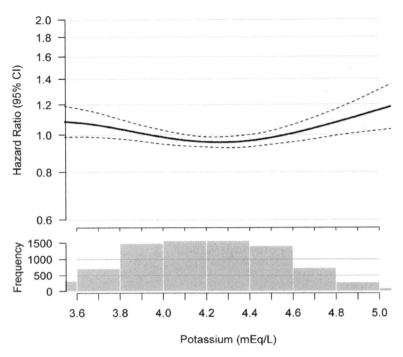

Figure 12: Functional form of serum potassium as a continuous variable with all-cause mortality in a pooled cohort of MESA and CHS participants. The upper figure presents the hazard ratios and 95% confidence intervals (95% CIs) for associations between milliequivalent per liter of serum potassium and all-cause mortality, adjusted for age, sex, race, time-varying eGFR, diabetes mellitus, systolic BP, study cohort (MESA versus CHS), current smoking, pack-years smoking, ever having had cancer, angiotensin-converting enzyme inhibitors/angiotensin II receptor blockers, diuretics (potassium sparing and all others), nonsteroidal anti-inflammatory drugs, potassium supplements, β blockers, β agonists, and other antihypertensive medications. The lower histogram presents the distribution of serum potassium concentrations in milliequivalent per liter for 9651 combined individuals from the MESA and CHS. CHS, Cardiovascular Health Study; MESA, Multi-Ethnic Study of Atherosclerosis.

The study was done on 9,651 individuals from the multiethnic study of atherosclerosis and the cardiovascular health study. All of these patients were free of cerebrovascular disease at baseline.

This study had several strong points. The study was fairly robust in the number of people that were followed. The follow-up time was 10.5 years, which is a relatively reasonable period of time for a follow-up.

The results of this study states, "Compared with serum potassium concentrations between 4.0 and 4.4 milliequivalents from those with concentrations greater than five, were at higher risk for all-cause mortality with a hazard ratio of 1.41." This is a very significant finding as the hazard ratio indicates a 41 percent increase in mortality risk. It is one of the reasons that the range of 4.0–4.4 mEq/L is chosen as the optimal health level.

One interesting aspect of this study is that it indicated that members of the population with a serum potassium of greater than 5.0 mEq/L, who were also concurrently using diuretics, were at higher risk of each negative end point compared with those who were not using diuretics.

Diuretic pharmaceuticals are things that make you urinate often, such as hydrochlorothiazide or Lasix, etc., and when they are combined with a slightly elevated potassium level, the result is increased mortality. It's important to remember that correlation is not causation, so we can't say for sure that using diuretics caused an increase in mortality. However, it does inform us that for patients that are using diuretics and have a slightly elevated serum potassium, we should watch carefully for other signs and symptoms.

Severe hyperkalemia, or high potassium, has been very well recognized as a causative factor in fatal arrhythmias, including ventricular fibrillation, asystole, and cardiac arrest. These are all terms for different forms of cardiovascular electrical transmission problems leading up to and including cardiac arrest.

- "Ventricular fibrillation" refers to an irregular heart rhythm where the lower heart chambers contract in a rapid and poorly coordinated manner causing decreased blood flow to the body.

- "Fibrillation" refers to an irregular rhythm of the heartbeat, which can often lead to blood clots and stroke.

- "Asystole" and "cardiac arrest" means the lack of electrical and mechanical activity of the heart. It is otherwise known as a "flatlining."

The graphs indicated a very strong U-shaped curve for mortality by potassium levels. What's very clear is that the range of 4.0–4.4 mEq/L has the lowest mortality risk. The ranges of 3.8–4.0 mEq/L and 4.4–4.6 mEq/L show only slight increases in mortality. But once the value drops below 3.8 mEq/L or exceeds 4.6 mEq/L, the increase in mortality is very significant.

This study gave us the opportunity to look at cause-specific death rate, as well as total mortality. Compared with the 4.0–4.4 mEq/L range, those with serum potassium between 4.5–4.9 mEq/L (again, well within the standard ranges that are used by most labs) were at a significantly higher risk for cancer. The odds ratio indicated a 23 percent increase in cancer death while there was an increase in all-cause mortality of 46 percent.

Among participants who used diuretics and had a serum potassium greater than 5.0 mEq/L, there was a 115 percent higher mortality risk. So that's well over double, if they used diuretics and had a higher serum potassium, even within the standard range.

So, again, this is a very good study, that is relatively easy to understand and has very clear graphs showing that 4.0–4.4 mEq/L range of serum potassium is the healthiest range.

POTASSIUM AND HIGH BLOOD PRESSURE

"Short-Term Mortality Risk of Serum Potassium Levels in Hypertension: A Retrospective Analysis of Nationwide Registry

Data"[32] is from the Danish National Registry and is a very robust study with 44,799 patients.

In this study, researchers were looking at patients that were hypertensive (high blood pressure), who were 30 years or older and had a serum potassium measurement during the time that they were in the study.

All-cause mortality was analyzed using seven predefined potassium levels, which is great because the more you can break it down, the better you can understand the significant differences in mortality with relatively minimal changes in potassium levels.

They used the range of 4.1–4.4mmol/L as the reference interval because that range had the lowest mortality rate of the seven strata.

Potassium:	Hazard ratio	Low 95%	High 95%	P
K: 2.9–3.4 mmol/L	2.80	2.17	3.62	<0.01
K: 3.5–3.7 mmol/L	1.70	1.36	2.13	<0.01
K: 3.8–4.0 mmol/L	1.21	1.00	1.47	0.05
K: 4.1–4.4 mmol/L	1	Reference		
K: 4.5–4.7 mmol/L	1.09	0.88	1.34	0.44
K: 4.8–5.0 mmol/L	1.48	1.15	1.92	<0.01
K: 5.1–5.8 mmol/L	1.70	1.20	2.41	<0.01
Age: 30–50 years	0.62	0.41	0.96	0.03
Age: 51–70 years	1	Reference		
Age: 71–80 years	1.89	1.57	2.28	<0.01
Age: >80 years	4.49	3.75	5.38	<0.01
Gender, Female	1.50	1.31	1.72	<0.01
Atrial fibrillation	1.34	1.14	1.57	<0.01
Acute myocardial infarction	1.12	0.91	1.36	0.28
COPD	2.02	1.71	2.38	<0.01
Stroke	1.44	1.21	1.70	<0.01
Heart failure	1.46	1.23	1.72	<0.01
Diabetes	1.05	0.85	1.31	0.64
Potassium supplements	0.92	0.81	1.06	0.25
ACEIs/ARBs & Beta blockers	0.84	0.58	1.22	0.36
Beta blockers & Thiazide diuretics & Potassium supplements	1.46	1.03	2.08	0.03
ACEIs/ARBs & Calcium channel blockers	1.03	0.68	1.57	0.87
Other single pill antihypertensive drug combinations	1.85	1.43	2.40	<0.01
ACEIs/ARBs & Thiazide diuretics	0.65	0.42	1.01	0.05
ACEIs/ARBs & Thiazide diuretics & Potassium supplements	1	Reference		

Figure 13: All-cause mortality in hypertensive patients stratified by potassium intervals (90-day follow-up). n = 44 799. Model adjusted for covariates. Reference interval represented by the interval K: 4.1–4.4 mmol/L; and single-pill combination of angiotensin-converting enzyme inhibitors/angiotensin receptor blockers, thiazide diuretics, and potassium supplements. ACEIs/ARBs, angiotensin-converting enzyme inhibitors/angiotensin receptor blockers.

Potassium	Hazard ratio	Low 95%	High 95%	P
K: 2.9–3.4 mmol/L	3.11	2.41	4.00	<0.01
K: 3.5–3.7 mmol/L	1.83	1.47	2.29	<0.01
K: 3.8–4.0 mmol/L	1.21	0.99	1.46	0.06
K: 4.1–4.4 mmol/L	1	Reference		
K: 4.5–4.7 mmol/L	1.16	0.94	1.42	0.17
K: 4.8–5.0 mmol/L	1.83	1.41	2.36	<0.01
K: 5.1–5.8 mmol/L	2.47	1.75	3.48	<0.01

Figure 14: All-cause mortality in hypertensive patients stratified by potassium intervals (90-day follow-up). n = 44 799. Reference interval represented by the interval K: 4.1–4.4 mmol/L.

For the patients with hypokalemia (that's on the low end of the range), the hazard ratio indicated a mortality rate of over three times the rate of death versus the baseline group. Even as we move up into more normal ranges, we still see an increase in deaths until we get up to the 4.1–4.4 mmol/L reference range. As we get above that range, we see the U-shaped curve (lying on its side) starting to take effect between 4.8 and 5.0 mmol/L. Again, these are within the so-called "standard ranges."

So, it's very clear that there's a U-shaped curve with an optimal value between 4.1 and 4.4 mmol/L.

POTASSIUM AND HEART FAILURE

The International Journal of Cardiology featured "Mild Hyperkalemia and Outcomes in Chronic Heart Failure: A Propensity Matched Study"[33] in which researchers were looking at increased mortality in chronic heart failure and the relationship of that mortality to serum potassium levels.

They had 7,788 chronic heart failure patients in a particular Digitalis (a pharmaceutical medication) Investigation Group trial.

It is quite clear, in this study, that potassium levels above 5.5 mmol/L are harmful in heart failure. It is pointed out that little was known about the safety of serum potassium levels between 5.0 and 5.5

mmol/L. The results indicate that mild hyperkalemia (high potassium) had a slight increase in mortality of seven percent as we start moving up into higher ranges that are still within "standard ranges."

Above 5.0 mmol/L, which is a mild hyperkalemia group, there was a 33 percent increase in mortality.

The conclusion of this study is that serum potassium, in this case between 4.0 and 4.9 mmol/L, is optimal and much safer than the standard values. However, it's important to point out that they did not run a group that was in a range of 4.0–4.4 mmol/L, which is our recommended optimal range. It simply indicated that higher levels of potassium above 4.9 mmol/L had higher mortality rates.

POTASSIUM AND HEART FAILURE, KIDNEY DISEASE, AND DIABETES

We recommend that you take a look at the study "Association of Serum Potassium with All-Cause Mortality in Patients with and without Heart Failure, Chronic Kidney Disease and/or Diabetes"[34] because of the meaningful graphs that appear. You will see eight full-color, beautiful U-shaped curves, which again support our optimal range of 4.0–4.4 mEq/L.

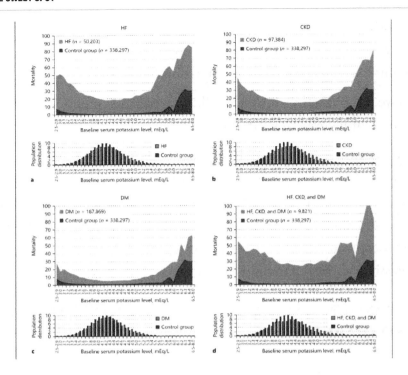

Figure 15: Unadjusted mortality (percent) over 18 months and histogram (percent) of serum potassium values per 0.1 mEq/L increments (2.5–8.0 mEq/L) in a: HF, b: CKD, c: DM, and d: combined cohort compared to controls. Data for patients with baseline serum potassium of 8.1–10.0 mEq/L are not reported because the sample size was small (n = 138). CKD, chronic kidney disease; DM, diabetes mellitus, HF, heart failure.

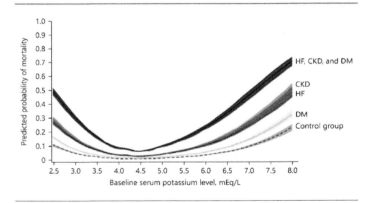

Figure 16: Spline analysis adjusted for covariates, showing serum potassium as a continuous variable with all-cause mortality over the distribution of potassium values (2.5–8.0 mEq/L) in HF, CKD, DM, and combined cohort compared to controls. Data for patients with baseline serum potassium of 8.1–10.0 mEq/L are not reported because the sample size was small (n = 138). CKD, chronic kidney disease; DM, diabetes mellitus, HF, heart failure.

One of the study's conclusions is this: "In summary, hypokalemia and hyperkalemia occurred commonly in a large, geographically diverse US population. Dyskalemia (which would include hypo and hyper) was associated with an increase in all-cause mortality over an 18-month follow up." Notice, this isn't even going out years. This is an 18-month follow-up. They saw a significant increase in mortality.

They're using a range under 5.0 mEq/L, but it's quite clear in looking at the graphs that 4.0–4.4 mEq/L is the ideal range.

POTASSIUM AND CARDIOVASCULAR HEALTH

In "Serum Potassium and Cardiovascular Mortality,"[35] the researchers are indicating, as many of these studies have, that there was not a lot of research looking at the impact of serum potassium on mortality. And so, the attempt here was to look a little deeper into the numbers to see what they could find in terms of cardiovascular health.

In this case, they put people into three groups in terms of range: the low was 2.7–3.7 mmol/L; the median was 3.8–4.4 mmol/L; and the high was 4.5–5.4 mmol/L.

The highest potassium range in this study, which was within most lab standard ranges, showed an increase in cardiovascular deaths of 8.1 percent (4.5–5.4 mmol/L) versus the median group.

The lowest potassium range in this study, which was within most lab standard ranges, showed an increase in cardiovascular deaths of 5.3 percent (2.7 – 3.7 mmol/L) versus the median group (3.8–4.4 mmol/L).

POTASSIUM AND STRESS

"The Importance of Potassium in Cardiovascular Disease"[36] has a very similar title to the study mentioned above. This study had different authors and a different group that was being observed.

The study indicates the importance of looking at the pivotal role of potassium in cardiovascular disease and the importance of preserving potassium balance.

The researchers argued that this was going to be a real "hot point," meaning there would be a lot of disagreement. They indicate that there's a lot of new and emerging information about cardioprotective and kidney protective therapies that promote potassium retention.

An important statement by the authors is that serum potassium values can vary widely on different blood tests, for a variety of reasons. The values can vary at different times of day if the blood is improperly handled, etc. They call it "pseudo hyperkalemia" or "fake high potassium."

The authors indicate that even things as simple as the prolonged use of a tourniquet above the site of the draw or even excessive fist clenching can change the values. The patient is often told to clench their fist before the blood draw, so that the phlebotomist can find the vein more easily.

They indicate that this could result in tissue hypoxia, or low oxygen, which can lead to the leaching of potassium from tissue into the plasma. This can cause an inaccurate serum plasma measurement.

So before going on drugs for low or high potassium, we recommend a retest, which you can order yourself through a variety of online labs for under $20, depending on the lab. We highly recommend getting retested if you're out of the optimal range.

This study has significant detail concerning the physiological issues that can cause either high potassium or low potassium and the types of kidney and gastrointestinal abnormalities, which can affect potassium levels. It is also pointed out that many medications can affect the potassium-to-magnesium balance.

Again, this is all indicative of these important interactions. It's the matrix. It's the contextual understanding that is often even more important than a single number.

Only two percent of total body potassium is within the extracellular (outside of the cells, and in the serum) fluid space. This means that tiny differences that might seem otherwise inconsequential can make a big difference in the outcomes of the lab tests.

They pointed out that in their study where they looked at patients with low magnesium and high potassium, those often parallel one another.

They looked at a thousand patients with hypokalemia or low potassium, and they found that 42 percent of those patients also had magnesium imbalances. We see again that all of these values must be examined and compared in order to make intelligent medical decisions. There's a huge checks-and-balances system at play in the body in general and in the blood.

HIGH POTASSIUM AND ELECTRICAL SYSTEM OF THE HEART

In "Electrocardiographic Manifestations of Hyperkalemia,"[37] the study's researchers pointed out that hyperkalemia is one of the more common, acute, life-threatening metabolic emergencies seen in an emergency department. So, potassium imbalances can lead to emergency room visits.

The researchers point to very specific complexes that show up on the electrocardiogram that can indicate problems in potassium intake. This is a study that won't appeal to most of the readers of this book, but we included it because it has some fascinating sidelights in it.

There's a study seemingly related to the above, entitled "Hyperkalemia—Induced Bundle Branch Block and Complete Heart Block."[38] Let's look at some of that language in the study's title:

- "Hyperkalemia" refers to high potassium.

- "Bundle branch block" means a change in electrical signaling within the heart.

  o There are many different grades of branch bundle block and types of branch bundle block.

  o Each grade and type have different levels of danger.

- "Complete heart block" is when electrical signals don't pass normally from the upper chambers of the heart to the lower chambers of the heart.

  o This is most commonly caused by a heart attack.

The researchers indicate that heart problems can continue even after potassium levels are balanced. They explain the manner by which potassium depresses certain conduction pathways and elements of the cardiac system to raise the possibility that hyperkalemia can induce a complete heart block.

POTASSIUM AND MORTALITY

The takeaway from the study entitled "Severe Hyperkalemia Requiring Hospitalization, Predictors of Mortality"[39] is that the mortality rate is higher in patients with normal baseline renal (kidney) function than in those with underlying chronic kidney disease.

This result is a little bit confounding and surprised the researchers as to why patients with a normal kidney function died at a higher rate than those with abnormal kidney function and high potassium levels.

This could be a result of understanding the etiology (causative factor) for high potassium caused by kidney failure, but not understanding the etiology of high potassium when there is no known kidney failure. Can you handle more? Here we go.

"A Propensity Matched Study of the Association of Low Serum Potassium Levels and Mortality in Chronic Heart Failure"[40] is a very valuable study to include, as it looked at more precise levels of potassium and mortality, than did most of the other studies.

In this study, researchers observed 6,845 patients, again in the Digitalis Investigation Group trial. Here is their conclusion: "In a cohort of ambulatory chronic systolic and diastolic heart failure patients, who were balanced and all measured baseline covariance, serum potassium less than four milliequivalents per liter was associated with increased mortality, with and a trend toward increased hospitalization."

Let's break that down:

- The phrase "cohort of ambulatory" refers to individuals who are actively moving around, but they do have a heart defect.
- "Systolic" is the highest number on blood pressure reading and it is when the heart is contracting.
- "Diastolic" is the lower number on blood pressure reading, the baseline pressure, when the heart is at rest.

When researchers balanced all the covariances, such as diabetes, obesity, alcohol use, smoking, etc., they found that a potassium level of lower than 4.0 mmol/L was associated with increased mortality.

So, this is a very significant study, again indicating an optimal potassium level between 4.0 and 4.4 mmol/L.

POTASSIUM AND DIURETICS

A study entitled "Non-Potassium—Sparing Diuretics and Risk of

Sudden Cardiac Death"[41] looked at the use of diuretics.

- Diuretics are pharmaceuticals that make you urinate and get rid of excess fluid.

- Some of the commonly used diuretics are non-potassium sparing.
  - They just make you urinate, and you lose potassium when doing so.

- There are also potassium-sparing diuretics that make you urinate but use a different methodology.
  - This category does not cause the loss of as much potassium.

The conclusions drawn from this study are as follows: "Current evidence supports the hypothesis that diuretic-induced potassium loss causes sudden cardiac death in some hypertensive patients. It seems prudent to use thiazide diuretics at a low dose only. Adding a potassium-sparing diuretic drug may further reduce the mortality risk."

So, what they're saying is that those hypertensive patients that are on a non-potassium-sparing diuretic have higher rates of sudden cardiac deaths because of the effect on potassium levels. They're saying that it's really important to use that type of diuretic at a very low dose.

If a patient needs higher dosages of diuretics, it seems that they should add potassium-sparing diuretics.

"Diuretic Therapy for Hypertension and the Risk of Primary Cardiac Arrest"[42] is a very similar study to the one mentioned above. In this case, the researchers were looking at very similar issues, but they quantified the amount of thiazide therapy or diuretic therapy.

They compared a low-dose therapy of 25 milligrams daily with a moderate-dose therapy, which they considered 50 milligrams daily. The moderate-dose therapy was associated with what they called a "moderate increase in risk" with an increase in mortality of 70 percent.

To us, that's a very large increase in risk. It's almost double. However, when they went up to a high-dose therapy of 100 milligrams a day, there was an increased risk of 260 percent.

Thiazide Dose	Single-Drug Therapy		Single- or Multiple-Drug Therapy	
	Case Patients/ Controls	Odds Ratio (95% CI)	Case Patients/ Controls	Odds Ratio (95% CI)
25 mg	5/35	1.0	8/51	1.0
50 mg	35/134	1.5 (0.5–4.9)	52/197	1.7 (0.7–4.5)
100 mg	8/23	3.5 (0.8–14.5)	18/54	3.6 (1.2–10.8)

*Data shown are for thiazide therapy regardless of the use of potassium supplementation. Odds ratios are adjusted for age, sex, pretreatment systolic blood pressure and heart rate, duration of hypertension, current smoking, and diabetes mellitus. $P = 0.07$ and $P = 0.02$ by the test for linear trend for patients treated with single and single or multiple drugs, respectively. CI denotes confidence interval.

Figure 17: Daily dose of thiazide therapy and the risk of primary cardiac arrest in patients with hypertension, according to the number of antihypertensive drugs.

That's almost four times the likelihood of dying from a primary cardiac arrest when a person is on diuretic therapy at high doses for hypertension. The table above also indicates that this increase occurs *regardless* of supplementation with potassium.

POTASSIUM AND BLOOD PRESSURE

The title of the study entitled "Potassium Citrate versus Potassium Chloride in Essential Hypertension Effects on Hemodynamic Hormonal and Metabolic Parameters"[43] includes great terms:

- "Hemodynamic" means how the blood flows through the blood vessels, which affects blood flow. It flows fastest where there is less friction.

- "Hormonal" refers to the effect of hormones, which are

produced in one location and transported to other areas in the body to stimulate specific cells.

- "Metabolic parameters" means the individual cardio-metabolic markers such as body mass index, cholesterol, blood pressure, glucose, and insulin resistance.

This type of study is called a "washout study," where the groups alternate the use of two different supplements. For example, group A takes drug X for four weeks, while group B takes drug Z for the same four weeks. The groups then switch, and group A takes drug Z, while group B takes drug X.

Researchers were looking to see whether an increase in potassium supply influenced blood pressure as well as influencing metabolic and hormonal issues.

What they found is that after eight weeks of potassium citrate intake, the systolic and diastolic pressures were reduced significantly. The mean decrease in pressures was about 6.2 millimeters of mercury. That may not sound like much, but just a one millimeter increase or decrease in blood pressure levels can actually have a very profound effect when you look at a large population.

In the potassium chloride group, there was a small insignificant reduction. So, obviously, they're recommending potassium citrate over potassium chloride.

POTASSIUM AND CARDIOVASCULAR DISEASE

"Serum Potassium and Risk of Cardiovascular Disease"[44] offers another look at the famous Framingham heart study. In this study, researchers are observing serum potassium concentrations and the effective risk for cardiovascular disease in a community-based population, meaning people that are not hospitalized.

We're looking at patients over 55, and when the age is over 70, we see even stronger correlations. In this study, the mean age was 43 years.

- Quartile 1 was 3.5 – 4.4 mmol/L

- Quartile 2 was 4.5 – 4.7 mmol/L

- Quartile 3 was 4.8 – 5.1 mmol/L

- Quartile 4 was 5.2 – 6.2 mmol/L

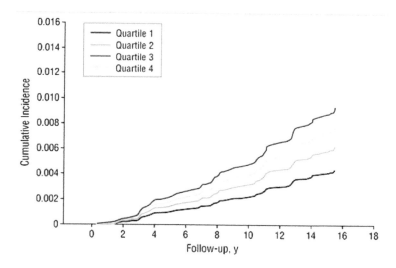

Figure 18: Age- and sex-adjusted cumulative incidence of death due to all causes according to quartile of serum potassium in 3151 individuals free of cardiovascular disease at baseline.

Here's the conclusion: "In our community-based sample of individuals free of cardiovascular disease and not taking medications that affect potassium homeostasis, serum potassium level was not associated with risk of cardiovascular disease."

It seems as though for younger people, the 4.0–4.4 mmol/L guideline that we are recommending may be slightly less important. We could look at a range of possibly 3.8–4.8 mmol/L without undue risk in a younger population.

POTASSIUM AND ATHEROSCLEROSIS

In the study entitled "Serum Potassium Mortality and Kidney Outcomes in the Atherosclerosis Risk in Communities Study,"[45] the researchers were looking at the association between different:

- Serum potassium levels and mortality

- Kidney outcomes

- Whether potassium-altering medications modify the associations

What they found was that "[h]yperkalemia was significantly associated with mortality, with a hazard ratio of 1.24, but less with some other conditions."

The conclusion was that:

- Higher values of serum potassium were associated with a higher risk of mortality in the general population.

- On the other hand, lower levels of potassium were associated with adverse kidney outcomes and mortality among patients that were not taking potassium-wasting diuretics.

So, here we're looking at different problems with low potassium versus high potassium levels. These correlations had been seen clinically but are now being confirmed with the research.

POTASSIUM AND SODIUM RATIO

One of the major values of "Sodium and Potassium Intake: Effects on Chronic Disease Outcomes and Risks"[46] is that it is a robust study. It is a meta-analysis looking at most of the large databases (including PubMed, Embase, Cochrane Database of Systematic Reviews, and others), so there was a very large amount of data to compare.

This study looked at 15,912 unique citations. *A citation is a reference in a study that gives enough information to clearly identify the source of the information so that it can be found by the reader.*

The researchers weren't looking at patients but at 15,912 citations in 171 other studies, so this is about as robust a study you will ever see. What they found is that sodium-to-potassium ratios were extremely important.

In practice, we find that serum sodium-to-potassium ratios often give a great deal more important information than do absolute sodium levels or absolute potassium levels. This is because this ratio gives a much stronger look at what's happening hormonally and in the kidneys.

In the study, researchers found that dietary sodium reduction, of even a relatively small amount, was significant.

The takeaway in this study is the enormous number of studies cited and investigated and the fact that the researchers concentrated on looking at sodium-to-potassium ratios, as opposed to each in isolation.

POTASSIUM AND ATRIAL FIBRILLATION

"Serum Potassium Levels and the Risk of Atrial Fibrillation: The Rotterdam Study"[47] found that atrial fibrillation is the most common sustained arrhythmia of the elderly.

Serum potassium is known to be associated with ventricular (associated with the lower and larger two chambers of the heart) arrhythmias and cardiac arrest, but little is known about the association of serum potassium with atrial (associated with the upper and smaller two chambers of the heart) fibrillation.

The researchers found that participants with hypokalemia (low potassium), in the more standard ranges of less than 3.5 mmol/L, had a 63 percent higher risk of atrial fibrillation. This was independent of age, sex, serum magnesium levels, and other confounders.

Simply having low potassium was associated with a higher rate of atrial fibrillation. *Atrial fibrillation is an irregular heart rhythm that can lead to blood clots.*

Patients with a prior myocardial infarction (heart attack) and low potassium have a 280 percent increased risk for atrial fibrillation.

POTASSIUM AND ARRHYTHMIAS

Now let's consider "Serum Potassium Levels and Mortality in Acute Myocardial Infarction."[48] In this clinical practice guideline, it was generally recommended to maintain a serum potassium level of between 4.0 and 5.0 milliequivalents per liter in patients who have experienced acute myocardial infarction. This clinical practice guideline was based on small studies that associated low potassium levels with certain types of arrhythmias.

This study showed a U-shaped relationship between post-admission serum potassium levels and in-hospital mortality that persisted after the adjustment for other variables.

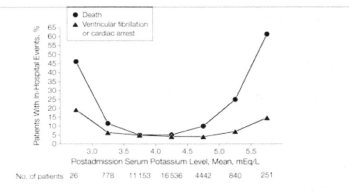

Figure 19: Each x-axis interval is equal to or greater than the lower limit of the interval and less than the upper limit. The first interval includes all serum potassium levels less than 3.0 mEq/L; the last interval includes all levels equal to or greater than 5 mEq/L.

The bottom line is that amongst patients with myocardial infarction, it was discovered that those who had post-admission serum potassium levels between 3.5 mEq/L and 4.5 mEq/L, had lower mortality levels —compared with those who had higher or lower potassium levels.

SUMMARY

- Much of the potassium research was conducted on patients with chronic kidney disease, hospitalized patients, and patients with acute medical conditions.

- Much of the potassium research was not done on a relatively healthy population.

- High potassium levels, above 4.5 mmol/L, have shown to have an increase in kidney disease, cardiovascular disease, and mortality risk

- Low potassium levels, below 3.9 mmol/L, have shown to have an increase in cardiovascular disease, muscle weakness, and increased mortality risk.

- In addition to looking at the potassium number, it is also important to look at the potassium-to-sodium ratio.

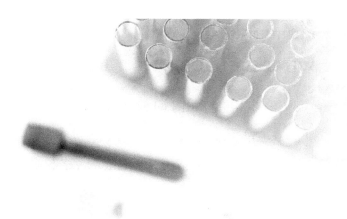

CHLORIDE

Major National Laboratory	96–106 mmol/L
Major HMO	100–111 mEq/L
Healthy Researched Values	102–105 mmol/L

FUN FACTS

- Chloride is one of the two components that make up table salt, along with sodium. This means that it's probably in most foods you eat.

- Chloride is derived from the element chlorine plus an electron.

- Chloride's name is derived from the Greek χλωρός (*chloros*), meaning "greenish yellow."

WHAT IS CHLORIDE?

- Chloride forms when chlorine (a halogen) gains an electron.

- Chloride is necessary for life.

- Chloride is an important electrolyte and one of the major minerals in the body. It makes up 0.15 percent of your total body weight.

- Most of the chloride is found in your blood and other extracellular fluids. Only about 15 percent is inside cells.

- Chloride is taken into the body through food and table "salt" intake.

- Most of the chloride is absorbed by the gastrointestinal tract, and the excess is excreted in urine.

FUNCTIONS OF CHLORIDE

- The levels of chloride in your blood are tightly controlled by the kidneys.

    o   They increase or decrease chloride excretion levels to compensate for short-term fluctuations in your chloride intake.

- Together with sodium and potassium, chloride is responsible for the fluid and acid-base (pH) balance in your body. As such, it's crucial for normal cell functioning.

- It contributes to the normal functioning of the digestive system in the stomach by contributing to stomach acid (hydrochloric acid).

- Chloride is important, along with sodium, in keeping normal levels of water in the body.

- Chloride often increases or decreases in direct relationship to sodium.

- Chloride levels may change without any change in sodium levels, when there are problems with too much acid or base in your body.

WHY MEASURE CHLORIDE?

- You measure chloride to determine if there is a problem with your body's acid-base balance and to monitor treatment.

- The normal blood level of chloride remains relatively steady, with a slight drop after meals (as the stomach produces acid after eating, using chloride from blood).

- A chloride blood test measures the amount of chloride in your plasma.

- You may also need a serum chloride blood test if you have symptoms of an acid or fluid imbalance, including:

  o Vomiting over a long period of time

  o Diarrhea

  o Fatigue

  o Weakness

  o Dehydration

  o Trouble breathing

WHAT DOES THE CHLORIDE TEST MEAN?

Serum chloride levels may be out of range for several reasons.

- High levels of serum chloride may be a sign of:

  o Dehydration

  o Kidney disease

  o Metabolic acidosis (too much acid in your blood)

- Low levels of serum chloride may be a sign of:

  o Heart failure

  o Lung disease

  o Addison's disease (low functioning of adrenal glands)

  o Metabolic alkalosis (too much base in your blood)

FROM DR. JOHN

In my practice, chloride is not a very exciting test. This is in opposition to sodium, which I could talk about for a day or even longer. I'll see wild fluctuations with sodium, and they're clinically relevant in my practice. I don't see that with chloride.

The reason for that is that my population, although they tend to be chronically ill, are not at death's door. I send a few people to the emergency room every year and quite a few people to urgent care. But for the most part, it's not a situation where they're in heart failure, etc. So, I don't see wild fluctuations in chloride very often.

So, that being said, I almost never even, by functional ranges, see high chloride. Or occasionally I see it, but never see extremely high chloride in a way that I feel threatened or concerned by it.

The research is quite clear, although there's not a lot of it. It's not like sodium research where there are thousands of papers. There's not so much research on chloride, but it's all consistent.

LOW CHLORIDE

Low chloride is a predictor of all-cause mortality and of cardiovascular mortality. High sodium is often a predictor of cardiovascular risk, and most people get their chloride in the form of sodium chloride (table salt).

It's rather interesting that sodium, if it's high, increases cardiovascular mortality risk, and chloride, if it's low, increases it.

LOW CHLORIDE AND CARDIOVASCULAR MORTALITY

The study "Is Low Serum Chloride Level a Risk Factor for Cardiovascular Mortality?"[50] looked at a risk ratio for cardiovascular disease mortality, for total mortality, etc.

This is what they found:

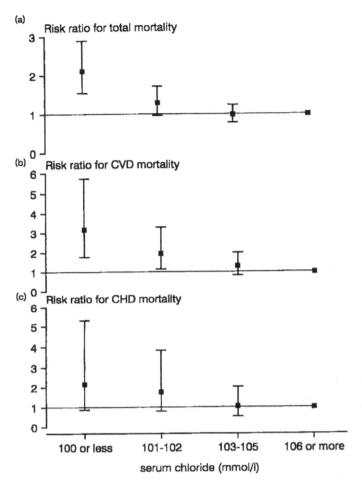

Figure 1: Associations between serum chloride levels at baseline and risk of total mortality (a), cardiovascular disease (CVD) mortality (b) and coronary heart disease (CHD) mortality (c) after 10 years of follow-up (BIRNH study).

- In patients whose chloride levels were less than 100 mmol/L, the mortality risk, from cardiovascular disease and congestive heart failure, was 5.5 times higher than 106 mmol/L or more.

- If they were at 101 to 102 mmol/L, their mortality risk was four times higher than 106 mmol/L or more.

  - This level of 101 to 102 mmol/L is within the "normal" range or "reference" range on the vast majority of laboratory tests, and yet, we see four times the mortality risk over the following 10 years.

- If they were at 103 to 105 mmol/L, the mortality risk dropped down to about two times higher than 106 mmol/L or more.

- And if their chloride level was higher than that, their risk continued to drop.

CHLORIDE AND MORTALITY

Another study that was published in the *Journal Hypertension*, "Serum Chloride Is an Independent Predictor of Mortality in Hypertensive Patients,"[51] used slightly different analysis methods, but essentially came to the same conclusions—low chloride is certainly a predictor of mortality in hypertensive patients.

There are not a lot of studies on chloride levels, but the studies that have been done are very consistent in showing that low chloride levels are generally dangerous. In most of the studies, it seemed difficult to determine if this is a function of causation or correlation.

We don't know if low chloride is causing the increase in mortality or if it's an indicator of a problem that is causing an increase in mortality. Either way, chloride levels should be more carefully monitored and evaluated using functional medical ranges.

SUMMARY

- It's very rare to have low or high chloride levels in otherwise healthy people.

- Low chloride levels are generally dangerous.

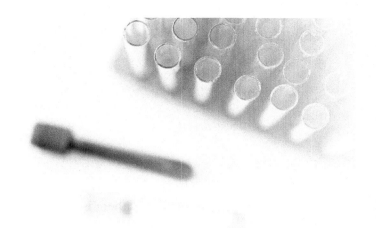

CARBON DIOXIDE/BICARBONATE

Major National Laboratory	20–29 mEq/L
Major HMO	24–33 mEq/L
Healthy Researched Values	25–28 mEq/L

AKA ...

The carbon dioxide blood test may be known by other names, including:

- Bicarbonate test
    - *Bicarbonate is the term used in most countries*
- Carbon dioxide content
- CO_2 content
- Total CO_2

- TCO_2
- HCO_3-
- CO_2 test-serum

FUN FACTS

- The CO_2 in our atmosphere is odorless and tasteless.
  - o It is at such a low concentration that we are accustomed to it.
  - o If the amount of CO_2 available in the air increased, we would notice a sharp acidic smell and taste.
- CO_2 is made of one carbon and two oxygen atoms.
- Carbon dioxide is frequently referred to as a greenhouse gas.
- The planet Venus's atmosphere consists of roughly 96–97 percent carbon dioxide.
- People and animals release carbon dioxide when they breathe out.
- Plants use carbon dioxide to make food in a process called photosynthesis.
- The properties of carbon dioxide were studied by the Scottish scientist Joseph Black (no relationship to the author) in the 1750s.

WHY TEST FOR CARBON DIOXIDE (AKA BICARBONATE TEST)?

- This is often a part of a collection of tests, which help investigate kidney health.
- You test for carbon dioxide to screen for an electrolyte or

acid-base imbalance.

- The bicarbonate test gives a rough estimation of acid-base balance.

- The test measures the total bicarbonate in the serum.

- Breathing brings oxygen (O_2) into the lungs with inhalation and releases carbon dioxide (CO_2) with exhalation.

- Blood carries CO_2 to the lungs, and it is exhaled without conscious effort.

- Bicarbonate may be measured along with sodium, potassium, and possibly chloride in an electrolyte profile. The ratio, or balance, of these as revealed in a test gives the most information.

WHAT DOES IT MEAN?

In a healthy individual, the level of CO_2 in the blood (actually bicarbonate) stays within a normal range and doesn't present any problems. However, if CO_2 levels rise too high or fall too low, it may be an indication of a health condition that needs to be addressed.

TOO MUCH CO_2 IN THE BLOOD COULD SUGGEST:

- Dehydration

- Frequent use of medications like antacids

- Lung conditions like pulmonary edema and chronic obstructive pulmonary disease (COPD)

- Diuretic (water pill) use, often in cardiovascular disease and high blood pressure

- Disorders affecting the adrenal glands like Cushing's disease (adrenal hormone excess)

- Impaired kidney function (This can also cause too little CO_2, as well.)

TOO LITTLE CO$_2$ IN THE BLOOD COULD SUGGEST:

- Hyperventilation, which causes respiratory alkalosis *(higher-than-normal levels of alkalinity in the blood)* and a compensatory metabolic acidosis *(too much acidity in the blood)*

- Excessive alcohol or drug consumption

- Thiamine (vitamin B1) deficiency

- Malnutrition

- Hyperthyroidism (overactive thyroid)

- Complications from type 1 or type 2 diabetes, such as ketoacidosis *(burning fats for fuel, rather than sugars)*

- Impaired kidney function

- Adrenal gland insufficiency such as Addison's disease

FROM DR. JOHN

Carbon dioxide, in my opinion, is another grossly underutilized test. When we're looking at a so-called "normal" or reference range for carbon dioxide, we're usually looking at a level between 20 and 29 mEq/L.

The recommended reference range, as indicated in this chapter, which is taken by analyzing the research given below, is intended to offer the healthiest functional medical range. That range is 25–28 mEq/L. So, you can see that's a big difference.

PLASMA BICARBONATE AND TYPE 2 DIABETES STUDY

"Plasma Bicarbonate and Risk of Type Two Diabetes Mellitus"[52] is a good study to start with in determining the healthiest levels for bicarbonate. Though it's about ten pages long, it's written in very clear language and is easy to understand. It also has some very easy-to-understand tables that are helpful as you are analyzing this information.

The study was done within the nurses' health study and contained 630 women. The researchers looked at about 60 different factors that could go into this increase in diabetes risk.

For the plasma bicarbonate (the bicarbonate that's carried in the blood), they quartiled the patients, or placed them in four groups, based on their bicarbonate levels. These are the four groups:

- Quartile one was a bicarbonate level less than 20.6 mEq/L.

- Quartile two was 20.6–22.3 mEq/L.

- Quartile three was 22.4–23.9 mEq/L.

- Quartile four was any level of bicarbonate over 23.9 mEq/L.

There was a significant difference in terms of lower diabetes risk in each of the quartiles as bicarbonate levels increased. In their interpretation, the researchers said, "Higher plasma bicarbonate levels were associated with lower odds of incident type 2 diabetes mellitus among women in the nurses' health study."

Again, this is a fun study because there's a lot of valuable information, and it's relatively easy to understand. They looked at a few other issues with the bicarbonate levels and they found, for example:

- The median level of bicarbonate in this cohort was 22.4 mEq/L.

- Women with plasma bicarbonate levels *above* the median had lower odds of diabetes than women with bicarbonate levels *below* the median. That's after they adjusted for all the matching factors.

SERUM BICARBONATE AND THE EFFECTS OF DRINKING SODA

Let's look at the study entitled "Lower Serum Bicarbonate and a Higher Anion Gap Are Associated with Lower Cardiorespiratory Fitness in Young Adults."[53] First, let's define some terms in the study's title:

- "Cardio" means the cardiovascular system.

- "Respiratory" represents the lungs, breathing, and gas exchange.

- "Serum bicarbonate" refers to the amount of sodium bicarbonate detected in the serum.

- "Anion gap" is simply the difference in levels between the positively and negatively charged electrolytes in the serum.

  o   A low anion gap indicates more alkaline, and a higher anion gap indicates more acidity.

What we're looking at here is the effect of low bicarbonate, which is an indicator of a higher acidic level. In addition, we are looking at a higher anion gap, which is a different measure of higher acidity in the blood. What is indicated in this study, is that there's a significant correlation between these two numbers (CO_2 and anion gap) and the cardiorespiratory fitness in young adults.

However, there are several other things that are even more interesting about this study. We know from a large body of work that chronic acidosis, or high acidic conditions in the body, have many different negative sequelae. There is a large body of work that clearly indicates that chronic acidosis in the body can lead to negative health outcomes.

Chronic metabolic acidosis can be a manifestation of chronic kidney disease, but it can also cause or be a causative agent for chronic kidney disease. It also contributes to insulin resistance, which can lead to diabetes and other negative conditions.

In this study, one of the interesting aspects is that they measured the changes in the serum bicarbonate levels and the anion gap after participants drank sodas. They had people, in some cases, drink sodas sweetened with sugar, and other groups were given artificially sweetened sodas.

What the researchers found was that drinking either of these two types of sodas caused acidosis or acidic conditions in the body.

Even in patients with well-preserved kidney function, there was increased phosphoric acid retention, which contributes to the increased anion gap (meaning higher acidity in the body).

Phosphoric acid is the ingredient, particularly in cola drinks but in other soft drinks as well, that gives you that explosion when you put it in your mouth. Phosphoric acid is what gives you that "ahhhh" feeling when you have that first sip of a cola drink.

Phosphoric acid and soda drinks lower bicarbonate levels and directly contribute to chronic kidney disease and diabetes. Although it is not indicated in this particular paper, we have considerable medical evidence that sodas and phosphoric acid also contribute to osteoporosis.

CO$_2$ AND INFLAMMATION

One of our favorite studies looking at bicarbonate and serum anion gap levels is "Serum Anion Gap, Bicarbonate and Biomarkers of Inflammation in Healthy Individuals in a National Survey."[54]

This study was looking at individuals without diagnosed disease. Their numbers in all the measured lab values were within what is generally considered "normal limits" though many of them were outside functional range limits.

The data suggested that lower extracellular pH (outside the cells, which would include the serum pH) activates the immune system. So again, lower pH indicates lower bicarbonate levels and more acidity. The study excluded people with chronic disease, infection, or kidney problems.

What they looked at was quite interesting. They looked at the mean values of the serum anion gap, bicarbonate levels, leukocyte counts, and C-reactive protein.

- Leukocytes are white blood cells, which are monitored as signs of infection or inflammation.
- C-reactive protein is a measure of systemic inflammation.

In this study, all of the patients were well within the normal ranges, or "normal limits." They divided the anion gap levels into quartiles, or four distinct groups. The study indicated that those in the quartile with the highest anion gap (more acidic) had a higher level of infection and/or inflammation (as indicated by high leukocytes) and inflammation (as indicated by the higher C-reactive protein levels).

This result was also found to be true of bicarbonate levels. As the bicarbonate levels decreased (indicating more acidity), levels of white blood cells and C-reactive protein increased.

Also, and this is quite interesting, we see that when a higher anion gap and lower bicarbonate level were both present, *again indicating an acidic condition*, there was a higher serum platelet count.

High serum platelets can be indicators of inflammation and of an increase in tendency of blood clotting. In our next book, you'll see that this elevation in platelet levels can be a strong indicator of increased mortality and death, so it is an extremely important measure that is often overlooked.

According to the study, the lowest level of anion gap (again indicating a more balanced pH and serum bicarbonate level) was 8.5 nanomoles per liter with a sodium bicarbonate level of 25.4 millimoles per liter. Those healthy levels are what they called their "target level" or "quartile one."

In that quartile one (or target level) we see:

- The body mass index was significantly lower.

- The serum albumin was lower, which in this case was beneficial.

- The serum creatinine was lower, which is beneficial and indicates better kidney health.

- The serum uric acid was significantly lower at 294.5 µmol/L versus 317.7 µmol/L in the fourth quartile.

CO_2 AND MORTALITY RATE

Let's take a look at the "Bicarbonate Concentration, Acid Base Status and Mortality in the Health, Aging and Body Composition Study."[55] First, we recommend that you don't use this as the first research study you try to investigate. It's very complex, long, and hard to follow, but we're going to give you the gist of it.

This study associated a healthy range of serum bicarbonate as anything over 23 mEq/L. They additionally indicated that a bicarbonate level over 32 mEq/L also created some fascinating difficulties.

The study indicated that people with low bicarbonate levels (under 23.0 mEq/L) had an increased mortality of 24 percent, over a 10.3-year period. In the high bicarbonate levels (greater than 28.0 mEq/L), it wasn't quite as significant. It was only about a 17 percent increase in mortality. *Still not great.*

One of the researcher's comments was that low bicarbonate may also be a risk factor for chronic kidney disease and a decline in eGFR (estimated glomerular filtration rate or state of kidney effectiveness).

In the low bicarbonate category (less than 23.0 mEq/L), the cardiovascular mortality rate was 23 percent higher and the non-cardiovascular mortality rate was 15 percent higher. Again, both of these findings indicate that low bicarbonate is a significant indicator of multiple pathologies.

In the paper, they go on to discuss the numerous other physiological complications of having low bicarbonate or any condition where there is increased acidity. They also pointed to a targeted serum bicarbonate concentration of approximately 26 mEq/L as ideal.

CO_2 AND KIDNEY FUNCTION

In the study entitled "Low Serum Bicarbonate and Kidney Function Decline: The Multi-Ethnic Study of Atherosclerosis (MESA),"[56] patients with established chronic kidney disease and metabolic acidosis (high serum acidity as indicated by low bicarbonate levels) are associated with a more rapid progression of kidney disease.

This was a fairly large study of people with an eGFR (estimated glomerular filtration rate), greater than 60. In general, most health care organizations use less than 60 as the cutoff for kidney disease. Among the participants, there was rapid kidney function decline of greater than five percent per year with low bicarbonate levels.

- The average bicarbonate concentration in this group was 23.2 mEq/L. At that level, the reduction in kidney function was greater than five percent per year.

- In bicarbonate levels below 21 mEq/L, as compared to 23 to 24 mEq/L, the decline was about 35 percent higher.

Therefore, the conclusion is that lower serum bicarbonate concentrations are independently associated with rapid kidney function decline independent of other markers.

CO_2 AND MUSCLE STRENGTH

The research paper titled "Association of Serum Bicarbonate Levels with Gait Speed and Quadriceps Strength in Older Adults"[57] offers a very short study that's fairly fascinating for a variety of reasons.

One of the important things in the study is that the researchers used a lower range for sodium bicarbonate, below 23 mEq/L. *(You don't have to remember milliequivalents per liter. You're going to just look at the number 23 on your test.)*

They determined that there was a significant association between low gait speed (the speed at which you walk) and the peak torque (power generated) from the quadriceps (or thigh muscles).

There were very significant differences in the two groups. There was about a 40–50 percent change in gait speed and peak torque for serum bicarbonate below 23 mEq/L, compared to levels above 23 mEq/L. *So that, in itself, is very, very significant.*

Participants with serum bicarbonate levels of less than 23 mEq/L had the following:

- Higher body mass index (indicating obesity)
- Higher albumin levels (indicating possible liver disease)
- Higher incidence of diabetes
- They commonly had a glomerular filtration rate of under 60 (which indicates Stage 3A or worse chronic kidney disease).

SUMMARY

- There is a great deal of significance in reappraising the lowest value of serum bicarbonate that should be considered normal.
    - That level should be significantly lower than we see on most laboratory results.
- The difference between a lower limit for normal of 20 mEq/L and 25 mEq/L, as suggested by a functional medicine practitioner, indicates a huge variance in potential mortality, or increased likelihood of dying.
- The ranges that are generally used on laboratory tests are quite unsatisfactory to predict or use as indicators of current or future disease and illness.
    - Most of the research we've looked at has used about 23 mEq/L as the bottom of their ranges and showed significant problems below 23 mEq/L.
    - When you get down in the 20 or 21 mEq/L range, it becomes a significant problem.

- This is a test on which we've rarely, if ever, seen doctors make any distinction in the values when they're in the so-called "normal range." But to us, this is a very significant marker of health.

CALCIUM

Major National Laboratory	8.9–10.4 mg/dL
Major HMO	8.8–10.5 mg/dL
Healthy Researched Values	9.4–9.8 mg/dL

FUN FACTS

- Interestingly, calcium seems to come in fifth place wherever it goes:
    - Fifth most abundant element by mass in the Earth's crust (after oxygen, silicon, aluminum, and iron)
    - Fifth most abundant dissolved ion in seawater (after sodium, chloride, magnesium, and sulfate)
    - Fifth most abundant element in the human body (after oxygen, carbon, hydrogen, and nitrogen)
    - It is, however, the most abundant metallic element in

the human body, 99 percent of which can be found in our bones and teeth, about two pounds of it!

- Calcium is abundant on the Moon. It is present at about 70 parts per million by weight in the solar system.

- Natural calcium compounds are readily available in the form of calcium carbonate deposits, limestone, chalk, marble, dolomite, gypsum, fluorite, and apatite.

- The Romans used to heat limestone, which is calcium carbonate, to make calcium oxide.

  o The calcium oxide was mixed with water to make cement, which was mixed with stones to build aqueducts, amphitheaters, and other structures that survive to the present day.

- The element name "calcium" comes from the Latin word *calcis* or *calx*, meaning "lime."

- Though calcium has been known for thousands of years, it was not purified as an element until 1808 by Sir Humphrey Davy of England. Thus, Davy is considered to have discovered calcium.

FUNCTIONS OF CALCIUM

Calcium is one of the most important minerals in the body. It is essential for the proper functioning of the following:

- Muscle movement and contraction
- Nerves
- The cardiovascular system
- Blood clotting

- The release of hormones and enzymes

- Formation of bones and teeth

WHERE IS CALCIUM LOCATED IN THE BODY?

- About 99 percent of calcium in the human body is found in bones while the remainder circulates in the blood.

- Roughly half of the calcium is referred to as "free" and is active.

- The remaining half is "bound" calcium.

- This bound calcium is attached to albumin and other compounds and is metabolically inactive.

HOW IS CALCIUM REGULATED IN THE BODY?

Several hormones control blood calcium within a narrow range of values.

- Parathyroid hormone (PTH)
    o PTH causes calcium levels to rise.
    o PTH is produced by a group of small glands in the neck:
        o Near the thyroid gland
        o Stimulated by a decrease in "free" calcium
    o PTH causes the release of calcium from bone and decreases calcium losses from the kidneys, so that calcium levels rise.
    o PTH stimulates production of the active form of Vitamin D by the kidneys
- Vitamin D

- o   Generally, causes calcium levels to increase
- o   Is converted to a hormone, which causes intestinal proteins responsible for calcium absorption to be increased
- o   Increases calcium absorption in the intestine
- o   Decreases calcium lost from the kidneys in urine

- • Calcitonin
  - o   Calcitonin (an amino acid hormone) is produced and in the thyroid gland.
  - o   Secreted by the parafollicular cells of the thyroid gland.
  - o   Generally acts to reduce blood calcium, the opposite of Vitamin D and parathyroid hormone.

These hormones keep blood calcium at healthy levels even though maintaining that balance in the blood may cause calcium to be released from bones.

HOW CALCIUM IS ABSORBED IN THE BODY

Calcium absorption is dependent on the following:

- • Optimal acidity of the stomach
- • Amount of phosphate and magnesium present
- • Actual absorption occurs in the upper part of the small intestine.

Calcium affects the amount of protein absorption and helps move fats through the intestinal wall.

PURPOSE OF THE CALCIUM TEST

There are two primary tests to measure plasma calcium.

- The *total calcium* test measures both the free and the bound forms (such as that which is bound to albumin).
  - It is important to know the serum albumin level in order to properly interpret the calcium levels.
  - This is generally what is measured on a basic chemistry panel.
  - Albumin carries the calcium.
- The *ionized calcium* test measures only the free, metabolically active form.

Blood and urine calcium levels cannot measure the amount of calcium in the bones, although there are other tests such as Bone Reabsorption Assessment Urine Test, to check for elevated levels of bone loss. To measure a current status of bone density, a DEXA scan is helpful for this purpose.

WHY MEASURE CALCIUM?

Serum calcium is usually measured to screen for or monitor the following:

- Bone diseases
- Parathyroid disease
- Calcium-regulation disorders (diseases of the parathyroid gland or kidneys)
- Thyroid disease

THE SWEET SPOT

- Kidney disease
- And several other medical conditions

SIGNS AND SYMPTOMS OF HAVING TOO MUCH CALCIUM IN YOUR BLOOD (HYPERCALCEMIA) INCLUDE:

- More frequent urination
- Increased thirst
- Fatigue
- Headaches
- Nausea and vomiting
- Loss of appetite
- Constipation
- Abdominal pain

SIGNS AND SYMPTOMS OF HAVING TOO LITTLE CALCIUM IN YOUR BLOOD (HYPOCALCEMIA) INCLUDE:

- Muscle cramps, especially in your back and legs
- Dry, scaly skin
- Brittle nails
- Confusion
- Irritability or restlessness
- Depression

SEVERE HYPOCALCEMIA (VERY LOW LEVELS OF CALCIUM IN YOUR BLOOD) CAN CAUSE THE FOLLOWING SYMPTOMS:

- Tingling in your lips, tongue, fingers, and/or feet
- Muscle aches
- Muscle spasms in your throat that make it difficult to breathe
- Stiffening and spasms of your muscles (tetany)
- Abnormal heart rhythms (arrhythmia)

FROM DR. JOHN

All doctors and most patients are quite aware that calcium is a critical factor in health. However, in my opinion, there is not enough attention given to close evaluation of calcium levels. A common range that is generally used in functional medical analyses to determine ideal health conditions is a serum calcium range of 9.4–9.8 mg/dL.

As in most blood chemistry tests, the "standard range" can vary considerably between different labs. The lab that I primarily use for my tests, which is one of the largest labs in the country, uses a normal range of 8.7–10.2 mg/dL. However, some labs report values as low as 8.5 mg/dL and as high as 10.5 mg/dL as being in the normal range.

FUNCTIONAL CALCIUM VALUES

I have come to accept the 9.4–9.8 mg/dL range as being the ideal healthy range. This is partially from other practitioners and also from reading the actual research on this. The range of 9.4–9.8 mg/dL is based upon mortality risk for calcium values.

CALCIUM AND HYPERPARATHYROIDISM

The primary causes of extremely high calcium levels as seen in our general practice are hyperparathyroid conditions:

- "Hyper" means high or elevated or excess.

- "Para" means next to.

- And then, obviously, "thyroid" refers to the thyroid gland.

The parathyroids are four small glands that are located adjacent to the thyroid gland and the throat. If those parathyroid glands become diseased, they can produce excessive levels of parathyroid hormone.

Parathyroid hormone, Vitamin D, and a variety of other hormones do a little dance with calcium. They determine whether bone is being made or broken down, or if calcium is being taken out of the bones. The parathyroid hormones control how much calcium is being absorbed through the intestines. So, it's quite a complex little dance.

To reiterate, the primary reason for very high and even moderately high serum calcium levels is hyperparathyroidism. Many experts in the field feel that if there is a calcium level of 10.0 mg/dL or higher, you should always check parathyroid hormone levels.
Of note, the parathyroid hormone levels and calcium levels should always be checked at the same time.

It's very rare in a general clinic, such as Dr. John's, to see extremely low calcium levels, so we're not going to speak to that issue in this book. We're going to look primarily at the high calcium levels. Fortunately, we have some very, very informative research studies in that area.

CALCIUM AND MORTALITY RATE

"Serum Calcium and Survival in a Large Health Screening Program"[58] is a robust study that tested 33,000 individuals. The researchers were looking at mortality (death) and morbidity (illness), but primarily examining mortality risk in a group of men.

One of the results indicated that men that had a serum calcium level of over 9.8 mg/dL exhibited a 20 percent increased risk in mortality compared to those with lower serum calcium values. This study is the predominant reason that we and others have arrived at 9.8 mg/dL being the top of the normal range.

When the range got up to 10.2 mg/dL, there was about a 50 percent increase in mortality risk over a 10.8-year period.

CALCIUM AND METABOLIC SYNDROME X

We've seen a great deal of information about cholesterol levels as though they're the most significant metabolic risk factor other than adiposity (fatness) and body mass index. However, there are numerous markers, many of which we will be talking about in this book and in subsequent books, that are considered non-conventional cardio metabolic risk factors. Many of them are far more important and more predictive of future mortality than cholesterol.

The "Serum Calcium Levels Are Associated with Novel Cardio Metabolic Risk Factors and the Population Based CoLaus Study"[59] looked at a variety of such non-conventional cardio metabolic risk factors.

Among the less commonly studied factors considered in this study were fat mass leptin levels.

- Leptin is a hormone that has many important functions.
- The two primary functions are:
    - Turning on our ability to burn fat.
    - Telling us we're satiated after a meal.

- If leptin is suppressed, which can be from a variety of reasons (primarily high cortisol levels and stress), then the following can occur:

  o We don't know when we've had enough to eat.

  o We keep eating to the point of excess.

- Because of suppressed leptin levels, our body won't burn the fat that we put on from eating that excessively large meal.

This study also looks at LDL (low density lipoprotein) particle size, APLB (apolipoprotein B), high sensitivity cardiac C-reactive protein, uric acid, homocysteine, and GGT, as well as some other non-conventional (but extremely important) cardiometabolic risk factors.

Many of these tests can be run at very low cost. For example, GGT, homocysteine, uric acid, and high sensitivity cardiac C-reactive protein are all included in our basic blood panels that we run in our clinic.

Their conclusion is that serum calcium was associated with metabolic syndrome. Metabolic syndrome, often called metabolic syndrome X, is the combination of factors that often appear together, including:

- Increased body mass index

- Increased body fat levels

- Increased blood pressure

- Increased cholesterol levels

- Increased insulin resistance leading to diabetes

A side note: in about 1250 AD, one of our favorite Chinese medical practitioners wrote a book called "Pi Wei Lun: Treatise of the Spleen and Stomach." He laid out this entire metabolic syndrome and, fortunately, indicated the lifestyle changes and herbal treatment to help eliminate it.

This study found that serum calcium had a strong association with the metabolic syndrome and also with non-conventional cardio metabolic risk factors, including uric acid, homocysteine, and GGT.

The bottom line is that this study seemed to indicate multiple pathologies related to increased calcium levels. Increased calcium levels were strongly associated with and seem to be causative for insulin resistance and diabetes.

HIGH CALCIUM AND MORTALITY RATE

"Serum Calcium Level Is Associated with Metabolic Syndrome in the General Population"[60] is a study with very similar findings to the study above and indicated a high association of elevated serum calcium to increased mortality.

This association was maintained even after the exclusion of patients treated with hypertensive drugs. The increased mortality indicated in this study was not primarily caused by hypertension. It was primarily directly correlated to high levels of serum calcium. Once again, we're looking at a high range of healthy calcium levels of around 9.8 mg/dL. This seems to be the turning point for increased mortality and morbidity.

CALCIUM AND TYPE 2 DIABETES

In "Serum Calcium Is Independently Associated with Insulin Sensitivity Measured with Euglycemic-Hyperinsulinaemic Clamp in a More Community Based Cohort,"[61] the study's hypothesis that these researchers were testing was that altered serum calcium was a direct factor in increased type 2 diabetes risk.

Their conclusion was that the data supports the notion that endogenous calcium (your serum calcium, but not dietary calcium intake) may be involved early in the development of diabetes.

One important bit of data is that this effect is mediated primarily through insulin sensitivity on the cells and cellular receptor sites. This is a very significant finding because it indicates that the problem is not with defective (or low levels of) insulin secretion from the pancreas.

FUNCTIONAL LABS IN THE CLINIC

We've had quite a few patients with moderately elevated serum calcium. We use the term "moderately elevated" to indicate a serum calcium level between 9.8 and 10.2 mg/dL. We subsequently tested many of these patients for parathyroid problems and also measured Vitamin D3 levels.

We tested two forms of Vitamin D3:

- 25-hydroxy Vitamin D3
  - This is the common test when someone says they had their Vitamin D tested.
  - It is essentially the storage form of Vitamin D3.
  - It's the less active form of Vitamin D3.

- 1,25 dihydroxy Vitamin D (which is the active form of Vitamin D or calcitriol).

  o It is converted from 25-hydroxy Vitamin D3 (in the kidney).

  o The active form of D3 creates most of the beneficial effects.

  o Generally, it is called calcitriol.

The second most common cause of elevated serum calcium after hyperparathyroid problems are problems with Vitamin D metabolism. This is particularly from over-conversion of the less active form of Vitamin D3 to the calcitriol form. In every case that we can recall, we were able to find a cause for the elevated serum calcium.

CASE STUDY: CLINICAL PATIENT HIGH CALCIUM AND CANCER

One case in particular, was a female around 70 years old in generally good health but who showed persistent increases in calcium levels in the 10.0–10.2 mg/dL range. Her medical doctor was unconcerned. Dr. John ordered a combined serum calcium and serum parathyroid hormone test and found that she had elevated parathyroid hormone levels.

She was later examined and had film studies of her neck that indicated that she had a hotspot on a parathyroid and subsequently had a parathyroid cancer removed.

She later developed breast cancer. We can't know for sure if the breast cancer had any relationship to the elevated serum calcium levels, but elevated serum calcium levels have conclusively been implicated in increased cancer deaths as well as increased cardiovascular deaths.

Those findings are consistent with the first study that we talked about above. That study indicated a 50 percent overall increased mortality risk in the high serum calcium levels.

CALCIUM, VITAMIN C, AND VITAMIN K2

As a sidelight, there's an ever-increasing body of evidence showing the dangers of taking exogenous, or supplemental, calcium and Vitamin D, particularly in menopausal women.

Some studies seem to indicate a 30 to 33 percent increase in calcium deposition and cardiovascular mortality in women who take high doses of Vitamin D and calcium. This risk is generally thought to be mediated by the additional intake of Vitamin K2.

Vitamin K2 activates the matrix Gla protein that pulls calcium out of the soft tissue, like the arteries, and also assists another mechanism in depositing calcium into the bones and teeth.

SUMMARY

- All doctors and most patients are quite aware that calcium is a critical factor in health.

- A healthy range tends to be 9.4–9.8 mg/dL.

- Calcium is primarily stored in bone although it's only one of many factors involved in osteoporosis and bone health.

- It is important to take Vitamins K2 and D3 when taking a calcium supplement because they significantly reduce risk of osteoporosis and cardiovascular disease, including heart attack and stroke.

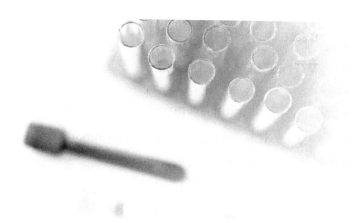

ALBUMIN

Major National Laboratory	4.1–5.2 g/dL
Major HMO	3.5–5.0 g/dL
Healthy Researched Values	4.5–5.0 g/dL

FUN FACTS:

- Chemical substance named for the Latin word for "the whites of eggs," where it occurs naturally.

- Etymology of "albumin" is from the 1590s Latin word *albumen (ovi)* "white (of an egg)," literally "whiteness," from the neuter of the Latin word *albus* "white."

  o The organic substance (which exists in egg whites) so called from the 1800s.[62]

WHAT IS ALBUMIN?

- Albumin is a protein made by your liver.

- It helps keep fluid in your bloodstream, so it doesn't leak into other tissues.

- It also carries various substances throughout your body, including:
    - hormones
    - vitamins
    - enzymes
    - bilirubin
    - calcium
    - progesterone
    - medicines

WHAT IS AN ALBUMIN BLOOD TEST?

- It measures the amount of albumin in your blood.

- An albumin blood test is a type of liver function test.

WHAT DO LOW ALBUMIN LEVELS INDICATE?

- Low albumin levels can indicate a problem with your liver or kidneys.

- It can indicate other less common medical conditions.

- Low levels of albumin can be caused by inadequate production of the albumin protein.

- Low levels can result from losing too much albumin in your urine or stool.

WHAT DO HIGH ALBUMIN LEVELS INDICATE?

- High levels may be a sign of dehydration.

- High levels may point towards liver disease, kidney disease, or an inflammatory disease.

- Higher albumin levels may be caused by acute infections, burns, stress from surgery, or a heart attack.

FROM DR. JOHN

Serum albumin, a protein that's synthesized in the liver, has been used historically as a marker of nutritional status. Serum albumin has powerful antioxidant properties.

Low serum concentrations have been suggested to be an indicator of a variety of conditions, including liver disease, hypercoagulation of the blood, and increased inflammation.

Higher serum albumin concentrations have been demonstrated to be inversely correlated with several risk factors for cardiometabolic disease.

Since albumin is a carrier for many of the chemicals and steroids in the body, it can impact the lab values for other items on the blood chemistry. If the albumin level is low, you have to carefully evaluate the other lab results.

For example, what may appear as a low calcium level may really be the result of a low albumin level. The albumin is not carrying enough calcium. In this example, there may be no need for additional calcium once the albumin level is normalized.

ALBUMIN AND CARDIOMETABOLIC HEALTH

In "Serum Albumin, Cardiometabolic and Other Adverse Outcomes: Systematic Review and Meta-Analyses of 48 Published Observational Cohort Studies Involving 1,492,237 Participants,"[63] one of the things to notice right off the top is this was a huge study.

This meta-analysis combines multiple studies, so it's going to give a broader cross-section of lifestyle, diet, ethnicity, and socioeconomics. It can help eliminate bias in one particular study or another and generally gives a more comprehensible picture.

In this study, we're looking at serum albumin ranges. The researchers divided the participants in these cohorts into three levels. The results, given in the image below, indicate that low serum albumin is a marker for increased risk of negative cardiometabolic outcomes.

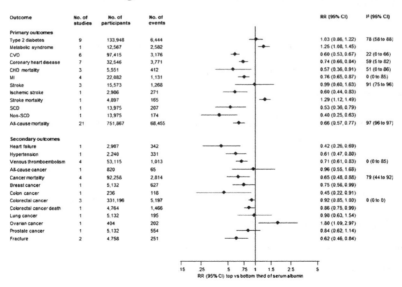

Figure 20: Summary associations of serum albumin with primary and secondary outcomes. CHD: coronary heart disease; CI: confidence interval (bars); CVD: cardiovascular heart disease; MI: myocardial infarction; RR: relative risk; SCD: sudden cardiac death; VTE: venous thromboembolism

Interestingly, the top third of albumin levels in generally healthy people is associated with reduced risk of cardiovascular disease, including:

- Myocardial infarction (heart attack)
- Stroke
- Heart failure (weakened function of the heart)
- Hypertension (high blood pressure)
- Cancer
- Breast cancer
- Colon cancer
- Colorectal cancer
- Fracture
- All-cause mortality

There was no significant association with diabetes, lung cancer, and prostate cancer.

The risk, however, was increased for ovarian cancer in the highest tertile. The researchers posited that the increase in ovarian cancer risk might have been because albumin, as a carrier of steroid hormones, may have increased hormone levels to the ovaries, possibly increasing the rate of ovarian cancer.

Personally, we would not necessarily leap to that conclusion, as the rates of breast cancer were lower in this group. We would think that if this result of increased ovarian cancer was being caused by increased hormonal delivery, the breast cancer risk should also be impacted.

ALBUMIN AND BLOOD SUGARS

In a study titled "Serum Albumin Levels Predict Vascular Dysfunction with Paradoxical Pathogenesis in Healthy Individuals,"[64] we see further evidence that albumin levels have a much narrower window as a marker of good health than was previously thought.

The researchers in this study placed the values in tertiles, or three different range groups. The results indicate a beautiful U-shaped relationship.

The highest tertile was 4.6–5.4 g/dL and indicated a 35 percent increased risk for high blood sugar in the upper tertile versus the middle tertile.

SUMMARY

- Serum albumin, which is a protein that's synthesized in the liver, has been used historically as a marker of nutritional status.

- Serum albumin has powerful antioxidant properties.

- Low serum concentrations have been suggested to be an indicator of a variety of conditions, including liver disease, hypercoagulation of the blood, cancer, and increased inflammation.

- Serum albumin concentrations have been demonstrated to be inversely correlated with several risk factors for cardiometabolic disease.

- Since albumin is a carrier for many of the chemicals and steroids in the body, it can impact the lab values for other items on the blood chemistry.

- If the albumin is low, you have to carefully evaluate the other lab results.

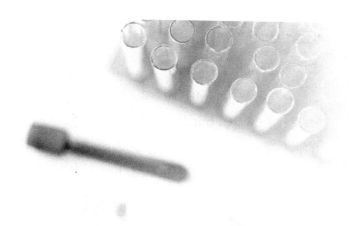

GLOBULIN

Major National Laboratory	1.5–4.5 g/dL
Major HMO	1.5–4.5 g/dL
Healthy Researched Values	1.9–3.0 g/dL

AKA …

- Serum globulin electrophoresis
- Globulin

FUN FACT

- Etymology of "globule" plus "in"—from the 1660s French word *globule*, meaning a "small, spherical body; little globe or sphere" and from the Latin word *globulus*, "a little ball," and the diminutive of *globus* or "round mass, sphere, ball."[65]

- Globulins are classified as globular proteins, known for their spherical shape.

- Most globulins are also identified by their inability to dissolve in water, but they dissolve readily in salt water.

- Gamma globulin is a class of globulins and a globular protein family identified by their position in serum protein electrophoresis.

- Immunoglobulins are the most significant gamma globulins.

- IgA, IgM, IgD, IgE, and IgG are gamma globulins.

- Biochemist J. Lawrence Oncley and associates created procedures to further purify gamma globulins and other proteins.[66]

- Gamma globulin rapidly replaced convalescent and animal sera for the prevention and treatment of infectious diseases such as measles, hepatitis, and polio. Then it came into widespread use as replacement therapy in the primary immune deficiencies, which emerged in the antibiotic era of the early 1950s.

WHAT ARE GLOBULINS?

- Globulins are proteins and are one of the three major blood proteins.

    o The major blood proteins are globulins, albumins, and fibrinogen.

- Globulins are a family of globular proteins that have higher molecular weights than albumin.

- Some globulins are produced in the liver while others are made by the immune system.

WHY TEST FOR GLOBULIN

- Globulins play important roles in liver function, blood clotting, and fighting infection.

- Measuring their levels can be used towards diagnosing a variety of conditions:

  o Liver damage or disease

  o Kidney disease

  o Nutritional problems

  o Certain autoimmune disorders

  o Certain types of cancer

WHAT DOES IT MEAN?

High globulin levels may indicate a likelihood, although not diagnostic by themselves, for the following:

- Certain types of blood cancers, such as multiple myeloma, Hodgkin's disease, or leukemia

- Hemolytic anemia

- Autoimmune diseases, such as lupus or rheumatoid arthritis

- Tuberculosis

Low globulin levels may be a sign of:

- Liver disease

- Kidney disease

FROM DR. JOHN

There is not a significant amount of information to be gleaned from the research information about perfect or ideal globulin levels. Part of the reason for that is that high or low globulins themselves are not a disease. They are an indication that there is a problem.

> It's like if the warning light goes off on your car, the warning light isn't causing the problem; it's telling you that you have a problem.

So, although high globulin levels can be indicators of inflammation, this inflammation could be a problem in kidney disease, liver disease, chronic infections, pancreatitis, or autoimmune problems. Several different cancers will show up with high globulin levels.

However, even within the standard ranges, we can look back at the A/G ratio (the albumin-to-globulin ratio) and see if there is a low albumin-to-globulin ratio. If there is an increased globulin or low albumin-to-globulin ratio, there would be concern of some type of serious inflammatory response.

A high A/G ratio (which could indicate low globulin) is often found in people with antibody deficiencies, inflammatory bowel diseases, some eating disorders, or an inability to absorb nutrients.

GLOBULIN, INFECTION, AND ALL-CAUSE MORTALITY

The name of the study featuring the graphs below is "Association of Serum Globulin with All-Cause Mortality in Incident Hemodialysis Patients."[67]

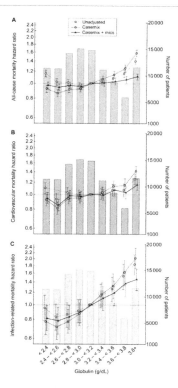

Figure 21: Associations of serum globulin (g/dL) with (A) all-cause, (B) cardiovascular and (C) infection-related mortality with hierarchical adjustments in 104,164 incident hemodialysis patients.

We are looking at these graphs at all-cause mortality and are seeing that the globulin numbers were quite important. Patients with a globulin concentration of greater than 3.8 grams per deciliter had a higher all-cause mortality, as well as infection-related mortality risk, than did those with a lower globulin concentration.

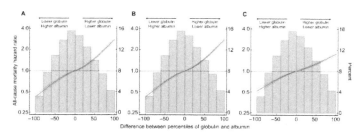

Figure 22: Mortality association of baseline globulin and albumin in 104,164 incident hemodialysis patients. (A–C) The sum of differences between percentiles of baseline serum globulin and albumin in (A) unadjusted, (B) case-mix, and (C) case-mix and MICS-adjusted

Patients with an A/G ratio of less than 0.75 had a 45 percent higher all-cause mortality hazard ratio. So once again, we're seeing that this value needs to be "in the pocket," neither too high, nor too low.

SUMMARY

- High or low globulin levels themselves are not a disease. They are an indication that there is a problem. It's like if the warning light goes off on your car, the warning light isn't causing the problem. It's telling you that you have a problem.

- High globulin levels can be indicators of inflammation.

  o This inflammation could be a problem in kidney disease, liver disease, chronic infections, pancreatitis, or autoimmune problems.

- Several different cancers will show up with high globulin levels.

- However, even within the standard ranges, we can look back at the albumin-to-globulin ratio and see that if there is a low albumin-to-globulin ratio, there is increased concern that there may be some type of serious inflammatory response.

- If it's a high albumin-to-globulin ratio, which could indicate low globulin, this is often a finding in people with antibody deficiencies, inflammatory bowel diseases, some eating disorders, or an inability to absorb nutrients.

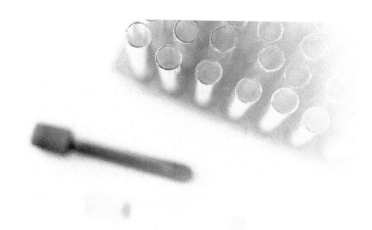

BILIRUBIN

Major National Laboratory	0.0–1.2 mg/dL
Major HMO	0.0–1.4 mg/dL
Healthy Researched Values	0.5–0.8 mg/dL

FUN FACTS

- Etymology of "bilirubin"—from the 1868 word *bili* for "bile" + Latin *ruber* for "red," meaning the "reddish pigment found in bile."

- In 1847, German scientist Rudolf Virchow and his associates isolated bilirubin crystals from hematomas and speculated that it was derived from blood. In 1950, Irving M. London and co-workers at Columbia University demonstrated that heme is indeed its source.[68]

- The bile pigment bilirubin is the major end product of the breakdown of heme in the liver.

WHAT IS IT?

- Bilirubin is a brown and yellow fluid that's a byproduct of the essential process of the breakdown of red blood cells (RBCs).

- One of the major functions of the liver is to break down old or damaged RBCs.

  o In this process, bilirubin is produced.

  o This substance is combined with others to make up bile (an essential fluid for digestion).

- Bilirubin is a major component of bile.

  o Bile is an important digestive fluid that has many uses of action.

  o Bile acts like a detergent to break apart large fat molecules.

  o Bile captures and carries many waste products through the colon for elimination.

  o Bile is created in the liver and stored in the gallbladder.

  o Bile is released into the small intestine, where it helps break down fats from food.

- Bilirubin gives solid waste products (feces) their characteristic color.

- There are two forms of bilirubin observed in the bloodstream.

  o Indirect bilirubin:

    - This form is insoluble, meaning it will not dissolve in water.

- It travels to the liver via the bloodstream, where it's converted to direct bilirubin, a water-soluble form.
  - Direct bilirubin:
    - This is the form bilirubin takes once it's been processed in the liver.
- Both forms of bilirubin—as well as total levels—are measured to help determine health status.

HIGH LEVELS OF BILIRUBIN

- Higher levels of bilirubin are evidence of potential problems such as:
  - Liver disease
  - Blockages of bile ducts
  - Arterial stiffness
  - Cardiovascular disease

LOW LEVELS OF BILIRUBIN

- Lower levels of bilirubin are evidence of potential problems such as:
  - A risk of coronary artery disease (CAD)
  - Increased risk of cerebral deep white matter lesions in the brain
  - Possibly seasonal depression

- o Diseases accompanied by non-hemolytic (not involving the breakdown of red blood cells) anemia

- o Blood vessel damage

FROM DR. JOHN

Bilirubin is a very interesting test that I believe is underutilized. The "normal range" is typically up to 1.2 mg/dL, and once it gets above that level, doctors will start to pay a little bit of attention, but they often don't pay much attention until it's even more elevated.

FUNCTIONAL VALUES OF BILIRUBIN

We are now seeing that the current levels of bilirubin that are considered normal are inadequate to assess future health and mortality risks. So, the functional levels recommended in this book are more consistent with "healthy values" that support greater health and lower future mortality.

These ideal values can vary from practitioner to practitioner, but the essential issue is to have a much narrower range than is shown in the current "normal" reference ranges. I believe that the research supports an ideal functional value for bilirubin of between approximately 0.5 to 0.8 mg/dL.

We will look at some studies where we see precisely why the 0.5 mg/dL is a very important marker for the lower range of normal. Once the value gets under 0.5 mg/dL, we see a significant increase in diabetes risk.

This increase in diabetes risk will, of course, eventually cause an increase in blindness, kidney disease, cardiovascular disease, liver disease, and death.

BILIRUBIN AND INFLAMMATION

In Dr. John's practice, anything over 0.8 mg/dL is a cause for attention. An elevated bilirubin level is often a sign of inflammation in the biliary tree, which includes the liver, the gallbladder, and the bile ducts, as well as surrounding tissues. Any level of inflammation in this area is something that deserves further exploration.

If a patient's bilirubin level is higher than 0.8 mg/dL, it's something we're going to check out. We're going to look into this more deeply because in many years, the number one surgery in the United States is gallbladder removal. In Dr. John's clinical experience, it is almost never necessary to remove a gallbladder if the lab values and physical symptoms are properly tracked and treated.

The real causes of gallbladder inflammation are generally overlooked in the medical community.

DIAGNOSTIC EXAM OF THE GALLBLADDER

In Chinese medicine, we have the great benefit of being able to take "pulses" at different positions on the wrist at the radial artery. There are multiple positions on each wrist. For each position, there are 27 possible pulse types that we may discern.

This combination of multiple locations and multiple pulse types yields thousands of possibilities in this matrix. This gives us a tremendous amount of information about internal organs and other conditions. Although this is something the medical science in the West currently has difficulty with, it's been used in countries throughout the East for over 2,500 years with great success. Pulse diagnostics can also be found in American medical textbooks written in the 1800s.

We can feel inflammation in the pulses. It is, in fact, possible to feel when gallstones are present in the gallbladder through the pulses. This sounds rather amazing, and Dr. John too was amazed when his mentor pointed out a gallstone pulse in him for the first time.

LOW BILIRUBIN

Low bilirubin has a variety of important impacts. There are a variety of conditions that can cause low bilirubin. However, in Dr. John's clinic it's very rare for me to find a low bilirubin level based on the "standard ranges." We will touch on this in some of the research studies.

In some of the research below, it was proven that low bilirubin levels can be a marker for diabetic retinopathy, or damage to the retina, caused by high blood sugars. In this condition, the blood vessels near the retina at the back of the eye are damaged. The study was not definitive concerning causation but indicated a strong correlation between low bilirubin and diabetic retinopathy.

LOW BILIRUBIN AND RETINOPATHY

According to one 2009 study, "Mortality Associated with Bilirubin Levels in Insurance Applicants,"[69] low bilirubin levels have been associated with retinopathy and have also been associated with blood vessel damage. While this study indicated correlation and not necessarily causation, we also understand that this type of blood vessel damage increases stroke risk.

In "Inverse Association Between Serum Bilirubin Levels and Retinopathy in Patients with Type Two Diabetes Mellitus,"[70] the type of diabetes the study looked at, type 2 diabetes, is an acquired form that is generally adult onset.

- "Retinopathy" simply means a pathology or illness of the retinas in the back of the eye.

- Retinopathy can eventually lead to blindness.

In the study researchers quartiled patients into four groups by their levels of bilirubin. There was a tremendous increase in microvascular (small blood vessel) disease in the time period leading up to a diagnosis of diabetes in the lowest quartile.

There are over 93 million people worldwide injured with retinopathy, which is a very severe condition.

In this study, it was found that:

- In patients who were diabetic but had no retinopathy, the total bilirubin tended to be about 0.65 mg/dL.

- Those with diabetes and retinopathy had an average bilirubin level of 0.47 mg/dL.

- It's important to remember that most labs and medical organizations consider low bilirubin to be under 0.3 mg/dL.

Here we are seeing that at the 0.3 mg/dL level, there is already a significant increase in diabetic retinopathy.

Showing the correlation between serum total bilirubin and severity of diabetic retinopathy.

	Quartiles of serum total bilirubin (mg/dl)				p-value
	<0.40	0.41-.50	0.51-.60	>0.61	
Controls	11	10	3	6	0.010
NO DR	2	6	5	11	
Mild NPDR	5	4	3	3	
Moderate NPDR	8	8	3	3	
Severe NPDR	7	1	0	1	
PDR	11	4	1	0	

Figure 23: Showing the correlation between serum total bilirubin and severity of diabetic retinopathy. NPDR (non-proliferative diabetic retinopathy), PDR (proliferative diabetic retinopathy), DR (diabetic retinopathy)

BILIRUBIN: THE MIGHTY CELL PROTECTOR

In the study called "Biliverdin Reductase, a Major Physiological Cytoprotectant,"[71] be aware that "cyto" means that it is involved with your cells and "protectant" refers to protecting your cells.

We can see that one important byproduct of bilirubin is biliverdin reductase.

- Biliverdin reductase is a byproduct of bilirubin.

- For years, biliverdin didn't really have any clear physiologic role.

- Biliverdin again arises from bilirubin, a product of the breakdown of red blood cells.

- We now find that biliverdin is a very potent antioxidant.

- Biliverdin can protect cells from a 10,000-fold (that's right— 10,000) excess of H_2O_2 (hydrogen peroxide, which can be very damaging to cells).

So, it's another case where we want to make sure that the level of bilirubin does not drop down even close to the 0.3 mg/dL level because it is the precursor to biliverdin.

When you're looking at lab tests, the *Journal of Insurance Medicine* is a really great place to look. These are the actuaries who compute the risk for anything. These companies make or lose money based upon their assessment of a patient's health coming into the insurance group, so they scan the research very carefully.

MORTALITY AND BILIRUBIN

The conclusion of the study entitled "Mortality Associated with Bilirubin Levels in Insurance Applicants"[72] was that isolated elevations of bilirubin, in a generally healthy screening population, were not associated with excess mortality.

However, values below the midpoint were associated with negative health outcomes. Other investigations have suggested a cardiovascular cause may underlie the excess mortality associated with low bilirubin.

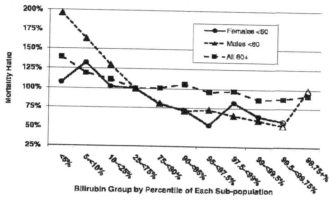

Figure 24: Mortality ratios for all cases with all other LFTs normal (95th percentile).

The chart above indicates a reverse J-shaped curve, which is quite interesting.

- In blood tests, a J-shaped or U-shaped curve will occur in almost all tests.

- There is always a sweet spot, which is at the bottom point of the curve where the lowest rate of mortality is indicated.

- We'll see the mortality risk going up in both directions around the sweet spots.

- Usually, it goes up faster on the right side of the arm, which indicates the elevation in chemical levels.

- However, in the bilirubin curve, the mortality curve is strongly weighted toward lower levels being actually more dangerous.

- *This means too low a level is more dangerous than too high a level in normal reference ranges.*

BILIRUBIN AND CORONARY ARTERY DISEASE

"Impact of Serum Bilirubin Levels on Carotid Atherosclerosis in Patients with Coronary Artery Disease"[73] is a study that provides good insight on the relationship between bilirubin levels and atherosclerosis. Let's break down the term "coronary artery disease":

- "Coronary artery disease" relates to the heart and arteries.

- "Carotid" indicates the major arteries up the front of the neck and into the brain.

- "Atherosclerosis" indicates a narrowing of the arteries, which can happen through a variety of disease processes.

The researchers in this study assumed that bilirubin protects against oxidative stress and stress-mediated diseases, particularly atherosclerotic diseases. What they find is that:

- Patients with carotid atherosclerosis have a high incidence of negative cardiovascular events.

- The researchers looked at the possible relationship between serum bilirubin levels and carotid atherosclerosis in patients with coronary artery disease.

The results were pretty dramatic.

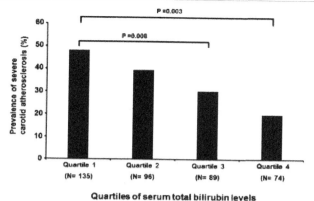

Figure 25: Association of total bilirubin levels with the prevalence of severe carotid atherosclerosis, defined as a plaque score of > 10. The prevalence of severe carotid atherosclerosis significantly decreased across quartiles of serum bilirubin levels as follows: quartile 1, 48.2%; quartile 2, 39.6%; quartile 3, 30.3%; and quartile 4, 27.0%; p for trend = 0.007.

- Quartile one included patients with bilirubin levels of *under* 0.5 mg/dL.

  - Remember that's the key number in functional medicine.

- Quartile two was 0.5 to 0.7 mg/dL

- Quartile three was 0.7 to 0.8 mg/dL

- Quartile four was *over* 0.9. mg/dL

As shown by the graph above, those who have a bilirubin under 0.5 have a much higher chance of being diagnosed with severe carotid atherosclerosis.

The level of severe atherosclerosis was 48.2 percent in quartile one, which was the low level of bilirubin of *under* 0.5 mg/dL. This can be compared to a 27.0 percent severe atherosclerotic risk for those that were *over* 0.9 mg/dL. Again, we're seeing a healthy range that is much tighter than what is indicated on most blood lab panels.

Table 2. Data regarding carotid ultrasonography.

Variables	Quartiles of serum total bilirubin levels				p, Trend
	Quartile 1	Quartile 2	Quartile 3	Quartile 4	
Max IMT (mm)	2.67 ± 0.95	2.33 ± 0.95	2.36 ± 1.05	2.27 ± 0.98	0.003
PS	9.9 ± 5.0	8.3 ± 5.1	7.8 ± 4.9	7.9 ± 5.9	0.002
PS severity					0.004
Normal (< 1.1)	2 (1.5)	6 (6.3)	3 (3.4)	7 (9.5)	
Mild (1.1–5)	18 (13.3)	18 (18.8)	28 (31.5)	18 (24.3)	
Moderate (5.1–10)	50 (37.0)	34 (35.4)	31 (34.8)	29 (39.2)	
Severe (> 10)	65 (48.2)	38 (39.6)	27 (30.3)	20 (27.0)	

Data are presented as mean ± SD or n (%).

IMT, intima–media thickness; PS, plaque score.

Figure 26: Data regarding carotid ultrasonography. Data are presented as mean ± SD or a n (%). IMT, intima-media thickness; PS, plaque score.

In looking at percentages for diabetes risk, there was 80 percent in quartile one versus 71.6 percent in quartile four for diabetes. This indicates low serum bilirubin is a predictor of higher diabetes risk.

BILIRUBIN AND ARTERIAL STIFFNESS

We'll look at a study entitled "Serum Total Bilirubin Is Inversely Associated with Brachial Ankle Pulse Wave Velocity in Men with Hypertension."[74]

- Pulse wave velocity is a test measuring changes in the pulse characteristic at the ankle.

- It is a marker for arterial stiffness.

- It is also a marker for cardiovascular disease.

In Chinese medicine, we feel these changes in the pulses where we are actually palpating the pulses in multiple anatomical positions for 27 different qualities, one of which is arterial stiffness. This research gives us some direct numerical evidence for pulse wave abnormalities associated with hypertension or high blood pressure.

Male subjects were placed in two groups based upon their pulse wave values. There was a direct relationship in which the lowest rate of bilirubin was found in the patients with the worst pulse wave velocities. Again, this indicates a pretty direct link between low bilirubin and cardiovascular and vascular problems.

HIGH BILIRUBIN AND MORTALITY

"Association of Total Bilirubin with All-Cause and Cardiovascular Mortality in the General Population"[75] was a very robust study of 37,234 adults.

This study demonstrated that "higher levels of bilirubin were independently associated with all cause and cause specific mortalities." This association with increased mortality was indicated even within "normal ranges" of bilirubin.

This would indicate that the current "normal" ranges for bilirubin do not adequately assess current and future states of health. This would seem to clearly indicate that a change should be made in the bilirubin values that are considered "normal."

SUMMARY

- We are now seeing that the current bilirubin levels that are considered normal are inadequate to assess future health and mortality risks.

- The functional bilirubin levels recommended in this book are more consistent with "healthy values" that support greater health and lower future mortality.

- These ideal values can vary from practitioner to practitioner, but the essential issue is to have a much narrower range than is shown in the current "normal" reference ranges.

- An ideal functional value for bilirubin is between approximately 0.5 mg/dL and 0.8 mg/dL.

- The bilirubin level of 0.5 mg/dL is a very important marker for the lower range of normal.

- Once the value gets under 0.5 mg/dL, we see a significant increase in diabetes risk. This may increase the risk in:

  o Blindness

  o Kidney disease

  o Cardiovascular disease

  o Liver disease

  o Mortality

- High bilirubin levels, defined in this book as a value of about 0.8 mg/dL, are associated with increased risk of:

  o Arterial stiffness

  o Cardiovascular disease

  o Liver disease

  o Blockages of bile ducts

ALKALINE PHOSPHATASE

Major National Laboratory	44–121 IU/L
Major HMO	25–100 IU/L
Healthy Researched Values	40–80 IU/L

AKA ...

- Alkaline phosphatase
- ALP
- Alk phos
- Alkaline phos

FUN FACTS

- Alkaline phosphatase (ALP) is also a member of the metallo-protein family of enzymes, which are *zinc dependent* for their optimal function.

- The principal clinical value of measuring serum alkaline phosphatase lies in the diagnosis of cholestatic liver disease (reduction or stoppage of bile flow).

  o Some of the highest elevations in alkaline phosphatases are present in patients with cholestasis.

- For those who study skeletal biology or treat and diagnose metabolic bone diseases, alkaline phosphatase could be considered one of their "favorite enzymes."

- It is one of the most frequently examined enzymes in all of medicine. Often this is because of its use for detection, follow-up, and investigation of skeletal disease.

- The term "alkaline phosphatase" emerged when it became necessary to distinguish "bone phosphatase" from the phosphatase in the prostate that features an acidic pH optimum.[76]

WHAT IS IT?

- Alkaline phosphatase is an enzyme.

  o Enzymes are a type of protein that catalyzes (causes or accelerates) chemical reactions in the body.

  o It helps break down proteins.

- The majority of alkaline phosphatase in serum (more than 80 percent) is released from liver and bone, and in small amounts from the intestine.

- Alkaline phosphatase has a half-life of seven days.

- Its clearance from serum is independent of bile duct patency or functional capacity of the liver.

- Alkaline phosphatase is known to contribute to the following processes:

  - Transporting nutrients and enzymes to and from the liver

  - Aiding in the development, growth, and maintenance of bone

  - Transporting calcium and phosphate from the intestines to bones, muscles, and nerve cells to ensure normal function

  - Transporting fatty acids to store energy in adipose (fatty) tissue and help maintain the structural integrity of cells

  - Regulating cell growth in fetuses during pregnancy

- It is normally present in high concentrations in bile and growing bones.

  - It is essential for the deposition of minerals in bones and teeth.

IF ALKALINE PHOS IS HIGH

- Elevated levels of ALP in the serum can be seen with any liver dysfunction.

- It could indicate cholestasis, either intrahepatic (inside the liver) or extrahepatic (outside the liver).

- It could indicate several types of cancers, including cholangiocarcinoma, pancreatic head adenocarcinoma, or ampullary adenocarcinoma.

- It could indicate choledocholithiasis (one or more gallstones in the common bile duct).

- It could indicate biliary stricture (narrowing of the bile ducts).

- It could indicate sclerosing cholangitis (disease of the bile ducts).

- ALP of bone is the most common extrahepatic (non-liver) source of increased ALP levels.

- ALP levels are high during childhood and puberty due to bone growth and development.

- In individuals with blood groups O and B, serum alkaline phosphatase levels increase after consuming a fatty meal, due to contribution from the intestinal tract.

  o As this elevation can persist for up to 12 hours in the serum, the recommendation is to check such people's serum enzyme levels in a fasting state.[77]

IF ALKALINE PHOS IS LOW

- It may be a sign of a lack of zinc.

- It could indicate malnutrition (poor food intake, poor dietary choices, or gut malabsorption).

- It could indicate pernicious anemia (anemia caused by a severe inability to utilize Vitamin B12).

- It could indicate thyroid disease.

- It could indicate Wilson's disease (disease of copper accumulation).

- It could indicate hypophosphatasia (low phosphate levels).

ALKALINE PHOSPHATASE AND MORTALITY

In "Associations Between Selected Laboratory Tests and All-Cause Mortality,"[78] there were multiple selected laboratory tests that were graphed according to mortality risk.

In this study, the only tests that were conclusively proven to have increased mortality, within the standard reference ranges, were:

- Blood urea nitrogen

- Albumin

- Alkaline phosphatase

The higher the alkaline phosphatase, the higher the positive association with mortality.

SUMMARY

- Alkaline phosphatase can be an indicator for many different disease processes.

- High or low alkaline phosphatase levels would indicate the need for further testing.

- It is important to note that mortality from several of these disease processes can be elevated within what are generally considered "standard reference ranges."

- For this reason, the recommended "healthy ranges" should be utilized as general health screening ranges.

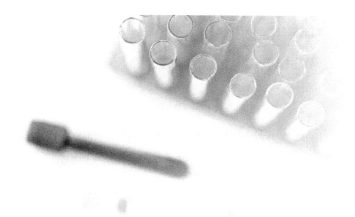

AST/ASPARTATE AMINOTRANSFERASE

Major National Laboratory	0–40 IU/L
Major HMO	10–40 IU/L
Healthy Researched Values	Men: 16–25 IU/L Women: 16–21 IU/L

AKA ...

- AST
- SGOT Serum Glutamic-Oxaloacetic Transaminase
- Aspartate aminotransferase

FUN FACTS

- Aspartate aminotransferase (AST) is an enzyme that catalyzes the transfer of amino groups between biologically active compounds, especially between aspartic acid and glutamic acid.

WHAT IS AN AST TEST?

- An AST test measures the level of aspartate aminotransferase.

- This enzyme is found in the liver, heart, brain, pancreas, muscles, and other tissues in the body.

- This enzyme helps the liver convert food into energy.

- A high AST on a blood chemistry test can be a sign that the liver or other cells in which it is contained may be injured or irritated, causing the enzyme to leak out of the given cells.

- When cells that contain AST are damaged, they release AST into the bloodstream.

- An AST blood test is often part of a routine blood screening to check the health of the liver and, to a lesser extent, other organs.

HOW IS ASPARTATE AMINOTRANSFERASE (AST) DIFFERENT FROM ALANINE TRANSFERASE (ALT)?

- Alanine transferase (ALT) is an enzyme that's commonly measured along with AST in a liver function panel or comprehensive metabolic panel (CMP).

- Both these enzymes can leak into the bloodstream when certain cells in the body are damaged.

- While both are known as liver enzymes, AST is found in more parts of the body than ALT. It is not as liver specific or as indicative of liver damage as ALT.

- Because of this, higher-than-normal levels of ALT tend to be a more specific indicator of liver conditions than higher-than-normal AST levels.

- Reviewing both these levels together when assessing the health of your liver is ideal.

- AST-to-ALT ratios can also be used to monitor for kidney pathologies.

AST AND LIVER DISEASE

In "Normal Serum Aminotransferase Concentration and Risk of Mortality from Liver Diseases: Prospective Cohort Study,"[79] the aminotransferases that are tested for are alanine aminotransferase, which is ALT, and aspartate aminotransferase, which is AST.

While I also mentioned this study in the upcoming ALT section, it is so important that I'm going to list it here as well.

Table 3 Relative risk of mortality by all causes by the serum aminotransferase concentration at baseline (expressed as floating absolute risks)

	Total No of Participants	All causes		Cancers		Cardiovascular diseases		Diseases of digestive system	
		No of deaths	RR* (95% CI)	No of deaths	RR* (95% CI)	No of deaths	RR* (95% CI)	No of deaths	RR* (95% CI)
Men									
AST (IU/l):									
<20	26 416	619	1.0 (0.9 to 1.1)	292	1.0 (0.9 to 1.1)	118	1.0 (0.8 to 1.2)	18	1.0 (0.6 to 1.6)
20-29	48 185	1 494	1.3 (1.2 to 1.4)	665	1.2 (1.1 to 1.3)	318	1.4 (1.2 to 1.5)	58	1.8 (1.4 to 2.4)
30-39	13 964	590	1.7 (1.6 to 1.9)	262	1.7 (1.5 to 1.9)	107	1.4 (1.2 to 1.7)	51	5.6 (4.2 to 7.3)
40-49	3 127	219	2.7 (2.4 to 3.1)	98	2.8 (2.3 to 3.4)	33	1.8 (1.3 to 2.5)	36	16.9 (12.2 to 23.5)
50-99	2 397	358	5.4 (4.9 to 6.0)	158	5.5 (4.7 to 6.4)	39	2.6 (1.9 to 3.6)	79	42.7 (34.1 to 53.6)
≥100	444	112	8.6 (7.2 to 10.4)	39	6.7 (4.9 to 9.2)	9	3.3 (1.7 to 6.4)	46	120.4 (89.2 to 162.5)

Figure 27: Relative risk of mortality by all causes by the serum aminotransferase concentration at baseline (expressed as floating absolute risks)

	Total No of Participants	All causes		Cancers		Cardiovascular diseases		Diseases of digestive system	
Women									
AST (IU/l):									
<20	25 362	185	1.0 (0.9 to 1.2)	104	1.0 (0.8 to 1.2)	28	1.0 (0.7 to 1.6)	1	1.0 (0.1 to 7.1)
20-29	19 463	174	1.0 (0.9 to 1.2)	113	1.2 (1.0 to 1.5)	22	0.7 (0.5 to 1.1)	2	2.3 (0.3 to 16.7)
30-39	2 114	24	1.2 (0.7 to 1.6)	12	1.0 (0.6 to 1.8)	2	0.4 (0.1 to 1.6)	2	18.5 (2.8 to 139.6)
40-49	336	3	0.8 (0.3 to 2.5)	3	1.5 (0.5 to 4.6)	0	—	0	—
≥50	247	8	2.9 (1.4 to 5.8)	3	2.1 (0.7 to 6.5)	0	—	3	—

Figure 28: Adjusted for age, body mass index, smoking status, alcohol consumption, plasma glucose, serum total cholesterol, blood pressure, and family history of liver disease.

In this study, they put people into six categories for AST levels:

- Under 20 IU/L
- 20–29 IU/L
- 30–39 IU/L
- 40–49 IU/L
- 50–99 IU/L
- Over 100 IU/L

They used that lower range of under 20 IU/L as their "reference range," so that would be given a value of 1.0.

The study looked at mortality or future chances of dying over the eight year follow-up period. They used the lowest level as the reference range. As that number went up, it was an indication of increased mortality.

In this study the number of deaths from all causes:

- At 20–29 IU/L mortality risk was 30 percent higher than the baseline level of under 20 IU/L.
- At 30–39 IU/L mortality risk was 70 percent higher than baseline.
  - It is important to remember that this level of 30–39 IU/L would be considered "normal" on many standard AST labs.
- At 40–49 IU/L mortality risk was a 170 percent higher risk.
- At 50–99 IU/L mortality risk was a *440 percent greater risk*.

Cancers and cardiovascular disease also showed very similar patterns of increased mortality for each quartile increase in AST levels.

AST AND HEART DISEASE

The study titled "Aspartate Aminotransferase or AST and Mortality in Patients with Ischemic Heart Disease"[80] was very interesting.

- "Ischemic" means that there is insufficient blood flow.

- Ischemic heart disease means there is insufficient blood flow to the heart muscle.

The researchers looked at quite a few risk factors to show that AST levels reflected changes in three-year mortality risk.

The study featured our old favorite, the U-shaped curve.

- Here we can see that the *sweet spot*, the point of lowest future mortality, was at the AST range of 21.1–23.1 IU/L.

- An AST level of 32–40 IU/L had a mortality risk that was more than double than the level from 21.1–23.1 IU/L.

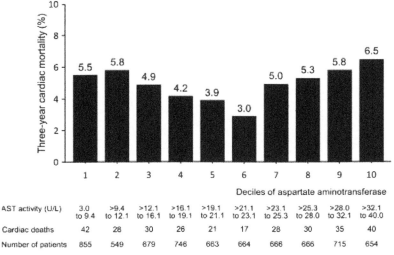

AST activity (U/L)	3.0 to 9.4	>9.4 to 12.1	>12.1 to 16.1	>16.1 to 19.1	>19.1 to 21.1	>21.1 to 23.1	>23.1 to 25.3	>25.3 to 28.0	>28.0 to 32.1	>32.1 to 40.0
Cardiac deaths	42	28	30	26	21	17	28	30	35	40
Number of patients	855	549	679	746	663	664	666	666	715	654

We can see from the above graphs that a perfect healthy range is between 21.1–23.1 IU/L.

By combining the ranges as indicated in the two graphs, we see that the upper graph indicates a perfect range of 21.1–23.1 IU/L while the same graph indicates that the value from 12–24.5 IU/L is a reasonably healthy range. This is where the "healthy/functional range" is derived for men.

The sweet spot is 16–24 IU/L in men, and 16–22 IU/L in women.

SUMMARY

- From these studies, we can see that the healthy range, indicating lowest future mortality risk, is much different than what was reported on most lab reports as being standard ranges.

- The range we have reported from one of the three largest lab testing companies indicated a "standard range" of 0–40 IU/L, which is extremely inaccurate as a predictor of future health and mortality.

- We see a striking increase in mortality when AST is below 12.1 IU/L in men.

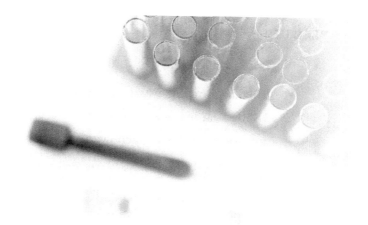

ALT/ALANINE AMINOTRANSFERASE

Major National Laboratory	0–32 IU/L
Major HMO	0–41 IU/L
Healthy Researched Values	13–22 IU/L for men 10–19 IU/L for women

AKA …

- ALT
- Alanine aminotransferase (ALT)
- Serum glutamic-pyruvic transaminase (SGPT)
- GPT

FUN FACTS

- Alanine aminotransferase (ALT) was formerly called serum glutamate-pyruvate transaminase or serum glutamic-pyruvic transaminase (SGPT).

- This amino acid was first synthesized by Adolph Strecker in 1850. Alanine was synthesized by combining acetaldehyde, ammonia, and hydrogen cyanide.

- Etymology: "*Alanin*" is German in origin, referring to "aldehyde." The German language uses the suffix *–in* for chemical compounds like English uses –ine.

- The term "alanine" was once named "alanin." It was later changed to "alanine."

WHAT IS IT?

- It is an enzyme found primarily in the liver and kidney.

    o An enzyme is a type of protein in a cell that acts as a catalyst and allows certain bodily processes to happen

- Normally, a constant low level of ALT exists in the serum.
- ALT levels can increase when liver cells are damaged.

    o ALT levels are used to screen for and/or monitor liver disease.

- It is often measured concurrently with AST as part of a liver function panel to determine the source of organ damage.

PURPOSE OF THE TEST

- The purpose of an ALT test is to assess the health of the liver.
- Damage to cells in the liver can cause ALT to leak into the bloodstream.
- ALT is commonly tested along with other liver enzymes and

compounds in the blood.

- These measurements combined can be used for diagnosis, screening, and monitoring of liver dysfunction.

- Taking multiple blood tests along with ALT provides more context for evaluating liver health.

- ALT can be used in conjunction with several other commonly ordered tests as a symptom, or predictor, of fatty liver disease.

- The formula for computing fatty liver disease can be found online.

HOW IS ALANINE TRANSFERASE (ALT) DIFFERENT FROM ASPARTATE TRANSFERASE (AST)?

- Aspartate transferase (AST) is another enzyme that's commonly measured along with ALT in a liver function panel or comprehensive metabolic panel.

- Both these enzymes can leak into the bloodstream when certain cells in the body are damaged.

- AST and ALT are both commonly considered liver enzymes.

  o There are greater amounts of AST in other parts of the body, such as the heart, skeletal muscles, and pancreas, as compared to ALT which is predominantly associated with the liver.

- ALT is more directly tied to your liver health, but both measurements are used to assess the health of your liver.

FROM DR. JOHN

As with many of the chemical markers we've been looking at and will look at in the future, the idea of how they should be used has shifted over time. One good example for that is alanine aminotransferase (ALT).

Two of the largest national labs in the United States, Quest and Labcorp, have extremely different healthy ranges for ALT. Neither of these laboratory ranges is consistent with the research cited in this book as effective for predicting and monitoring future health and mortality risk.

ALT's reference ranges were established in the 1940s and really have not been changed significantly since that time. Different health organizations and different labs have different value ranges for healthy ALT levels.

The high end of many standard reference ranges tends to be right around 40 IU/L, which was the original level set by the manufacturers, the makers of the ALT test. And it really hasn't adjusted much. Some labs indicate the top end of normal to be as high as 70 IU/L. So, it's a range that was really set approximately 80 years ago, which is before there was a complete understanding of what ALT does.

ALT is primarily a marker for liver damage, with damaged liver enzymes leaking out of damaged cells. It is still a very accurate marker for that type of cellular liver damage. However, the number that was set as the upper limit of normal, 40 IU/L, is much too high, as the following studies will indicate.

One of the things to notice if we're looking at a lab report is that we may see an ALT reference range of 0–40 IU/L. While we are looking at the high end as being very inaccurate, on the low end, it's even more inappropriate.

If a person has an ALT of zero, they won't have a functioning liver, as in *dead*. We must have some cellular activity. The range is very significant. And we find with ALT that the lower end of the range can also indicate some significant problems.

Liver diseases are increasing annually. You can go online and find apps for figuring out your own likelihood of having fatty liver disease. They call it "NAFLD," nonalcoholic fatty liver disease, but it doesn't matter if it's alcoholic or nonalcoholic. Just search for a "nonalcoholic fatty liver disease calculator," and you can plug in the numbers from your blood tests. It's a very, very easy procedure to see what your risk factor is for early-stage liver disease. Really helpful. Armed with these lower parameters, I've had many patients in whom we have detected liver anomalies at a very early stage.

Fortunately, our clinic regularly does individual and group liver cleanses, liver detoxes, etc., which can be very effective at healing the liver. It's actually astonishing to find what comes out of people's bodies during these cleanses.

Chinese medicine is quite famous for herbs that treat the liver effectively. It's really critical to address these conditions early before they've done significant damage and the problem moves beyond fatty liver into fibrosis or cirrhosis. Make sure you're taking these values very seriously and see someone who will treat you for liver conditions while you are still in a healthy range.

I could have listed any number of ways the liver can be damaged, from alcohol overuse to high fructose corn syrup users. In fact, a very high percentage of the population of teens are running around with fatty liver disease due to drinking Big Gulps, which have a great amount of fructose that is very damaging to the liver.

One of the reasons alcohol has historically been the primary cause of fatty liver disease is because it was one of the primary ways that people could get excess fructose into their system.

Fructose is broken down by a completely different system in the body than glucose is. The body is a highly tuned glucose refinery. There are multiple hormones involved in the breakdown of glucose for energy, but fructose is lacking those systems.

So, if there's too much fructose ingestion, the liver can't completely break it down, and some of it gets stored in the liver, as fat globules. Eventually when you get enough fat globules, you have a fatty liver.

So, we're seeing huge increases in fatty liver, nonalcoholic fatty liver disease, and it's primarily through fructose ingestion although there are many other factors involved.

FUNCTIONAL RANGES OF ALT AND CHRONIC LIVER DISEASE

Wu and colleagues' "Updated Thresholds for Serum Alanine Aminotransferase Level in a Large Scale Population Study Composed of 34,346 Subjects"[81] is a very robust study, due to an enrollment of over 30,000 patients.

The researchers began the study by saying that the background level of sensitivity of the current upper limit of normal for ALT levels, for detecting chronic liver disease, has been challenged recently.

These researchers reference another article that was done in Korea by Kang and colleagues[82] who had already revised their upper limit of healthy serum ALT to 31 IU/L for men and 23 IU/L for women.

While functional medical practitioners will generally use lower ALT values than those used in the Kang study, they indicate movement in the right direction. The values that we use, as supported by the research, is an ALT of 13–22 IU/L for men and 10–19 IU/L for women.

In Wu's study, it is pointed out that there were several large prospective studies. Those studies indicated that serum ALT levels greater than 20 IU/L were correlated with significantly higher rates of mortality from liver disease than did their counterparts with an ALT of less than 20 IU/L.

Another study conducted by Siddiqui and colleagues[83] also demonstrated that patients in the high/normal ALT range (between 20–40 IU/L) had higher incidences of developing complications of cirrhosis of the liver than patients with ALT levels of less than 20 IU/L.

They also mentioned that rates of hepatocellular carcinoma were higher with the higher levels of ALT, where:

- "Hepato" refers to the liver.
- "Hepatocellular carcinoma" means liver cancer.

A study by Kumada[84] demonstrated that a serum ALT level above 20 IU/L was an independent risk factor associated with the development of liver cancer.

These are very significant findings. In their conclusion, the researchers indicated that "the thresholds of upper limit of normal, of serum ALT levels should be lower to 24 for men and 17 for women to detect more unhealthy subjects and for optimal discrimination between healthy and unhealthy status."

This quote underlines and supports our premise for significantly lowering the ranges for ALT that are considered normal and healthy ranges. It also supports our premise that different ranges are appropriate for women than for men.

REVISING ALT LEVELS

In a study titled "Determination of the Upper Limits of Normal Serum Alanine Aminotransferase (ALT) Level and Healthy Turkish Population,"[85] once again, researchers were looking for the specific level that should be considered the upper limit to be used as a reference range for "normal ranges."

They're not even saying the "healthiest limits." The indication is if it's beyond this level, we need to do further testing. They indicated that we need to do a much deeper dive into the problem. Their conclusion was that the upper limit of normal should be lowered in men to 32.10 IU/L and to 23.15 IU/L for women.

ALT AND LIVER DISEASE

In "Normal Serum Aminotransferase Concentration and Risk of Mortality from Liver Diseases"[86] that we looked at in the previous section on AST, the researchers assumed that an ALT level of 40 IU/L was too high, and they set out to prove that conjecture.

The objective was to examine the relationship between the standard range of serum ALT and mortality from liver disease. This was a fairly comprehensive study where they quartiled the participants into four groups. This was a very thorough study and yielded some quite alarming results.

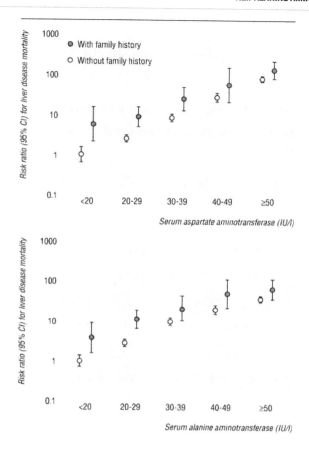

Figure 27: Association between serum aminotransferase concentration and mortality from liver disease in men by presence of family history of liver disease (expressed as floating absolute risks)

This study was not just regarding ALT. It was looking at ALT and AST. I'm going to report on the ALT aspect here. An ALT value of under 20 IU/L was given a reference range of 1.0, meaning that they would compare the other quartile groups to that number.

As the relative risk went up, the future mortality rate went up.

- In the 20–29 IU/L group, the relative risk indicated a 20 percent increase of mortality above the reference range.

- Comparing quartile 1 to quartile 3, which had a range of

30–39 IU/L, there was a 70 percent increase in mortality.

- Frighteningly, quartile 4, the 40–49 IU/L group, had an increased rate of mortality of 120 percent.

- ***This is frightening, as at least one national laboratory has this value of 40–49 IU/L included in their normal reference range.***

In looking at cancer risk, the relative risk in ALT showed the following in these quartiles and ranges:

- Quartile 2 (20–29 IU/L) showed an increase in mortality by 20 percent above the reference range.

- In quartile 3 (30–39 IU/L), the risk was observed to have increased by 60 percent above the reference range.

- Quartile 4, with a range of 40–49 IU/L, indicated a 110 percent increased risk above the reference range.

		All causes		Cancers		Cardiovascular disease		Diseases of digestive system	
	Total No of Participants	No of deaths	RR (95% CI)	No of deaths	RR (95% CI)	No of deaths	RR (95% CI)	No of deaths	RR (95% CI)
Men									
AST (IU/L)									
<20	26 416	619	1.0 (0.9 to 1.1)	292	1.0 (0.9 to 1.1)	118	1.0 (0.8 to 1.2)	18	1.0 (0.6 to 1.6)
20-29	48 185	1 494	1.3 (1.2 to 1.4)	665	1.2 (1.1 to 1.3)	318	1.4 (1.2 to 1.5)	58	1.8 (1.4 to 2.4)
30-39	13 964	590	1.7 (1.6 to 1.9)	262	1.7 (1.5 to 1.9)	107	1.4 (1.2 to 1.7)	51	5.8 (4.2 to 7.5)
40-49	3 127	219	2.7 (2.4 to 3.1)	98	2.8 (2.3 to 3.4)	33	1.8 (1.3 to 2.5)	18	16.9 (12.2 to 23.5)
50-99	2 997	358	5.4 (4.9 to 6.0)	138	5.5 (4.7 to 6.4)	39	2.6 (1.9 to 3.6)	79	42.7 (34.1 to 53.6)
≥100	444	112	8.6 (7.2 to 10.4)	39	6.7 (4.9 to 9.2)	9	3.3 (1.7 to 6.4)	46	120.4 (89.2 to 162.5)
ALT (IU/L)									
<20	57 425	1 061	1.0 (0.9 to 1.1)	494	1.0 (0.9 to 1.1)	197	1.0 (0.9 to 1.2)	34	1.0 (0.7 to 1.4)
20-39	36 589	1 197	1.2 (1.1 to 1.3)	535	1.2 (1.1 to 1.3)	263	1.3 (1.2 to 1.5)	61	2.1 (1.6 to 2.7)
30-39	11 975	516	1.7 (1.5 to 1.8)	215	1.6 (1.4 to 1.8)	85	1.5 (1.0 to 1.6)	60	6.9 (5.4 to 9.0)
40-49	4 068	225	2.2 (1.9 to 2.5)	93	2.1 (1.7 to 2.6)	38	1.7 (1.2 to 2.3)	40	13.5 (9.9 to 18.5)
50-99	3 887	310	3.0 (2.7 to 3.4)	133	3.1 (2.6 to 3.6)	32	1.4 (1.0 to 2.0)	72	23.4 (18.5 to 29.6)
≥100	589	83	5.2 (4.2 to 6.4)	44	6.2 (4.6 to 8.3)	9	2.9 (1.5 to 5.6)	21	41.0 (26.7 to 63.1)

AST = aspartate aminotransferase, ALT = alanine aminotransferase

Figure 28: Relative risk of mortality by all causes by the serum aminotransferase concentration at baseline (expressed as floating absolute risks).

AST = aspartate aminotransferase. ALT = alanine aminotransferase

Women

AST (IU/l):									
<20	25,362	185	1.0 (0.9 to 1.2)	104	1.0 (0.8 to 1.2)	28	1.0 (0.7 to 1.6)	1	1.0 (0.1 to 7.1)
20-29	19,463	174	1.0 (0.9 to 1.2)	113	1.2 (1.0 to 1.5)	22	0.7 (0.5 to 1.1)	2	2.3 (0.3 to 16.7)
30-39	2,114	24	1.2 (0.7 to 1.6)	12	1.0 (0.6 to 1.8)	2	0.4 (0.1 to 1.6)	2	18.5 (2.8 to 139.6)
40-49	336	3	0.8 (0.3 to 2.5)	3	1.5 (0.5 to 4.6)	0	—	0	—
≥50	247	8	2.9 (1.4 to 5.8)	3	2.1 (0.7 to 6.5)	0	—	3	—
ALT (IU/l):									
<20	35,187	257	1.0 (0.9 to 1.2)	154	1.0 (0.8 to 1.2)	32	1.0 (0.6 to 1.6)	2	1.0 (0.3 to 4.0)
20-29	10,201	103	1.2 (1.0 to 1.4)	62	1.2 (0.9 to 1.5)	17	1.3 (0.8 to 2.2)	2	2.7 (0.7 to 11.8)
30-39	1,380	19	1.4 (0.9 to 2.2)	11	1.4 (0.8 to 2.6)	3	1.3 (0.4 to 4.1)	0	
40-49	365	10	3.0 (1.6 to 5.6)	6	3.1 (1.4 to 6.8)	0	—	2	75.0 (19.7 to 314.7)
≥50	389	5	1.2 (0.5 to 3.0)	2	0.9 (0.2 to 3.5)	0	—	2	80.8 (19.7 to 314.4)

AST=aspartate aminotransferase. ALT=alanine aminotransferase.

Adjusted for age, body mass index, smoking status, alcohol consumption, plasma glucose, serum total cholesterol, blood pressure, and family history of liver disease

Figure 29: Relative risk of mortality by all causes by the serum aminotransferase concentration at baseline (expressed as floating absolute risks).

AST = aspartate aminotransferase. ALT = alanine aminotransferase

Adjusted for age, body mass index, smoking status, alcohol consumption, plasma glucose, serum total cholesterol, blood pressure and family history of liver disease.

Some of the more surprising numbers were in the results for digestive diseases. Under an ALT of 20 IU/L was given a baseline reference value of 1.0, and the following was observed:

- The mortality due to digestive diseases in the 20–39 IU/L group was indicated at a 110 percent increase.

- The third group, with the range of 30–39 IU/L (remember, this is still within the current "normal range" that most labs are reporting) had a relative risk of 6.9, nearly *7 times higher than the reference group.*

- When we examine the results for the 40–49 IU/L group, the relative risk was up to *13.5 times higher than baseline.*

These are astonishing numbers. Despite fairly small incremental changes in ALT levels, we see huge increases in digestive system diseases and mortality.

			Liver diseases		Liver cancer		Non-cancer liver diseases	
	Total No of participants	No of deaths	RR* (95% CI)	No of deaths	RR* (95% CI)	No of deaths	RR* (95% CI)	
AST (IU/l):								
<20	26 416	25	1.0 (0.7 to 1.5)	14	1.0 (0.6 to 1.7)	11	1.0 (0.6 to 1.8)	
20-29	48 185	108	2.5 (2.0 to 3.0)	76	3.1 (2.5 to 3.9)	32	1.7 (1.2 to 2.3)	
30-39	13 964	98	8.0 (6.6 to 9.8)	64	9.4 (7.4 to 12.0)	34	6.2 (4.4 to 8.7)	
40-49	3 127	70	25.7 (20.3 to 32.5)	44	29.5 (21.9 to 39.8)	26	20.8 (14.1 to 30.6)	
50-99	2 397	149	65.7 (55.8 to 77.4)	92	74.6 (60.7 to 91.8)	57	55.0 (42.2 to 71.7)	
≥100	444	51	111.3 (84.0 to 147.4)	17	65.4 (30.4 to 105.9)	34	167.2 (117.8 to 237.2)	

Figure 32: Relative risk of mortality from liver diseases in men by serum aminotransferase concentration at baseline (expressed as floating absolute risks)

AST = aspartate aminotransferase. ALT = alanine aminotransferase

ALT (IU/l)								
<20	37 425	45	1.0 (0.7 to 1.4)	27	1.0 (0.7 to 1.5)	18	1.0 (0.6 to 1.6)	
20-29	36 589	113	2.9 (2.4 to 3.5)	82	3.4 (2.8 to 4.3)	31	2.0 (1.4 to 2.8)	
30-39	11 975	110	9.5 (7.9 to 11.5)	64	9.3 (7.3 to 11.9)	46	9.9 (7.4 to 13.2)	
40-49	4 068	74	19.2 (15.3 to 24.2)	44	19.3 (14.3 to 26.0)	30	19.1 (13.3 to 27.4)	
50-99	3 887	117	30.0 (25.0 to 36.1)	69	30.2 (23.8 to 38.4)	48	29.6 (22.2 to 39.5)	
≥100	589	42	59.0 (43.4 to 80.1)	21	46.8 (30.4 to 72.1)	21	78.5 (51.0 to 120.9)	

AST=aspartate aminotransferase, ALT=alanine aminotransferase.

*Adjusted for age, body mass index, smoking status, alcohol consumption, plasma glucose, serum total cholesterol, blood pressure, and family history of liver disease.

Figure 33: Relative risk of mortality from liver diseases in men by serum aminotransferase concentration at baseline (expressed as floating absolute risks)

AST = aspartate aminotransferase. ALT = alanine aminotransferase

ALT AND METABOLIC DISEASE

In looking at "Normal Limit for Serum, Alanine Aminotransferase ALT Level and Distribution of Metabolic Factors in Old Population in Kalaleh, Iran,"[87] the study's conclusion was that the upper limit of normal for ALT should be considered to be far lower than the previously accepted value.

The study recommended that age, gender, ethnicity, and metabolic factors should be accounted for in future studies to determine a normal ALT level. This study is worth looking at, as it has a very clear U-shaped curve..

In summary, as given in the study: "Our current calculated upper normal limit of ALT, 21 IU/L in males and 19 IU/L in females respectively, is far lower than the generally accepted upper normal limit for ALT level, which had been determined by the laboratory manufacturer."

This is further confirmation for our two main points about ALT. An upper value of 21 IU/L is appropriate for men. An upper value of 19 IU/L should be used for women. This indicates in general a significant decrease in values considered as normal, as well as underlining the difference in values between men and women.

ALT AND CORONARY ARTERY DISEASE

The next study, "Inverse Association of Alanine Aminotransferase, ALT, within Normal Range with Prognosis in Patients with Coronary Artery Disease,"[88] looked at setting some of the lower limits for reference ranges. This study features a nice U-shaped curve. What the researchers indicated was the following:

- In the lowest quartile, which goes down to an ALT level of 2 IU/L, there was a 7.1 percent mortality in that group.

- When ALT is in the 17 IU/L range, mortality drops to 4.7 percent.

So, with cardiac mortality, having ALT that is too low is a significant problem.

This was a three-year study of cardiac mortality risk. Here we may be seeing the antioxidant effects and anti-atherosclerotic effects of having healthy levels of ALT.

The study entitled "Association between High-Normal Levels of Alanine Aminotransferase and Risk Factors for Atherogenesis"[89] shows the relationship of atherosclerotic disease of the cardiovascular system and ALT levels.

- "Atherogenesis" refers to the process of plaque formation leading to coronary artery disease.

- "Atherosclerotic disease" is a disease of the arteries character-ized by deposition of plaque of the inner wall of the arteries.

The study's aim is to show the relationship between ALT levels, liver disease, cardiovascular disorders, and numerous other metabolic dysfunctions.

In this study, there were a couple of interesting findings. Researchers analyzed a variety of markers and generally found that ***as ALT went up, basically all the good markers in the body went down, and all the bad markers went up***.

SUMMARY

- Liver diseases are increasing annually.

- You can go online and find apps for figuring out your own likelihood of having fatty liver disease.

- They call it NAFLD or nonalcoholic fatty liver disease, but it doesn't matter if it's alcoholic or nonalcoholic. Just search for a "nonalcoholic fatty liver disease calculator," and you can plug in the numbers from your blood tests.

- It's a very easy procedure to see what your risk factor is for early-stage liver disease. Really helpful. Armed with these lower parameters, we've had many patients in whom we have detected liver anomalies at a very early stage.

We have so many case studies on ALT, and it's really hard to pull up any single one. But once we became knowledgeable about these sig-nificantly lower levels of ALT and how they were dangerous, it shifted our view considerably.

The importance of catching pathologies early as opposed to trying to treat an end-stage disease is very evident with ALT levels, as well as with other lab markers.

Thus, the End of the Book ...

We would first like to thank you for reading this book. We hope that it can assist in bringing great health to a great many people.

This book is to let others know when they are outside the perfect, healthy target range, and when to take early action.

Nothing in this book should be considered a criticism or indictment of standard laboratory values as they have been used in general medical practice. Those values are extremely useful and relevant for moderately severe and very severe conditions. This book is really directed at those who wish to aim for maximum health.

Be Happy, Be Healthy!

ENDNOTES

1. Temple, R. (2013). *Genius of China: 3000 Years of Science, Discovery & Invention* (3rd ed.). Andre Deutsch.

2. Zhou, L., Mai, J.-Z., Li, Y., Wu, Y., Guo, M., Gao, X.-M., Wu, Y.-F., Zhao, L.-C. and Liu, X.-Q. (2019), Fasting glucose and its association with 20-year all-cause and cause-specific mortality in Chinese general population. *Chronic Diseases and Translational Medicine, 5*: 89-96. https://doi.org/10.1016/j.cdtm.2018.08.001

3. The DECODE Study Group, on behalf of the European Diabetes Epidemiology Group (2003). Is the Current Definition for Diabetes Relevant to Mortality Risk From All Causes and Cardiovascular and Noncardiovascular Diseases? *Diabetes Care, 26*(3), 688–696. https://doi.org/10.2337/diacare.26.3.688

4. Wei, M., Gibbons, L. W., Mitchell, T. L., Kampert, J. B., Stern, M. P., & Blair, S. N. (2000). Low fasting plasma glucose level as a predictor of cardiovascular disease and all-cause mortality. *Circulation, 101*(17), 2047–2052. https://doi.org/10.1161/01.cir.101.17.2047

5. Borch-Johnsen, K., Colagiuri, S., Balkau, B., Glümer, C., Carstensen, B., Ramachandran, A., Dong, Y., & Gao, W. (2004). Creating a pandemic of prediabetes: the proposed new diagnostic criteria for impaired fasting glycaemia. *Diabetologia, 47*(8), 1396–1402. https://doi.org/10.1007/s00125-004-1468-6

6. Nichols, G. A., Hillier, T. A., & Brown, J. B. (2008). Normal fasting plasma glucose and risk of type 2 diabetes diagnosis. *The American Journal of Medicine, 121*(6), 519–524. https://doi.org/10.1016/j.amjmed.2008.02.026

7. Bjørnholt, J. V., Erikssen, G., Aaser, E., Sandvik, L., Nitter-Hauge, S., Jervell, J., Erikssen, J., & Thaulow, E. (1999). Fasting blood glucose: an underestimated risk factor for cardiovascular death: Results from a 22-year follow-up of healthy nondiabetic men. *Diabetes Care, 22*(1), 45–49. https://doi.org/10.2337/diacare.22.1.45

8. Shin, J. Y., Lee, H. R., & Lee, D. C. (2011). Increased arterial stiffness in healthy subjects with high-normal glucose levels and in subjects with pre-diabetes. *Cardiovascular Diabetology, 10*, 30. https://doi.org/10.1186/1475-2840-10-30

9. Hu, G., & Duncan, A. W. (2013). Associations between selected laboratory tests and all-cause mortality. *Journal of Insurance Medicine, 43*(4), 208–220. https://www.ncbi.nlm.nih.gov/pubmed/24069781

10. Aronson, D., Mittleman, M. A., & Burger, A. J. (2004). Elevated blood urea nitrogen level as a predictor of mortality in patients admitted for decompensated heart failure. *The American Journal of Medicine, 116*(7), 466–473. https://doi.org/10.1016/j.amjmed.2003.11.014

11. Lind, L., Zanetti, D., Högman, M., Sundman, L., & Ingelsson, E. (2020). Commonly used clinical chemistry tests as mortality predictors: Results from two large cohort studies. *PLOS ONE, 15*(11), e0241558. https://doi.org/10.1371/journal.pone.0241558

12. Delanghe, J. R., & Speeckaert, M. M. (2011). Creatinine determination according to Jaffe—what does it stand for? *NDT Plus, 4*(2), 83–86. https://doi.org/10.1093/ndtplus/sfq211

13. Ostermann, M., Kashani, K., & Forni, L. G. (2016). The two sides of creatinine: both as bad as each other? *Journal of Thoracic Disease, 8*(7), E628–E630. https://doi.org/10.21037/jtd.2016.05.36

14. National Kidney Foundation. (2015, March 11). *Global Facts: About Kidney Disease.* https://www.kidney.org/kidneydisease/global-facts-about-kidney-disease

15. Said, S., & Hernandez, G. T. (2014). The link between chronic kidney disease and cardiovascular disease. *Journal of Nephropathology, 3*(3), 99–104. https://doi.org/10.12860/jnp.2014.19

16. American Chemical Society. (2020, November 30) *Molecule of the Week Archive: Uric acid.* https://www.acs.org/molecule-of-the-week/archive/u/uric-acid.html

17. Hassan, W., Shrestha, P., Sumida, K., Thomas, F., Sweeney, P. L., Potukuchi, P. K., Rhee, C. M., Streja, E., Kalantar-Zadeh, K., & Kovesdy, C. P. (2022). Association of Uric Acid–Lowering Therapy With Incident Chronic Kidney Disease. JAMA Network Open. 5(6), e2215878. https://doi.org/10.1001/jamanetworkopen.2022.15878

18. Desideri, G., Castaldo, G., Lombardi, A., Mussap, M., Testa, A., Pontremoli, R., Punzi, L., & Borghi, C. (2014). Is it time to revise the normal range of serum uric acid levels? *European Review for Medical and Pharmacological Sciences, 18*(9), 1295–1306. https://pubmed.ncbi.nlm.nih.gov/24867507/

19. Nakagawa, T., Mazzali, M., Kang, D. H., Sánchez-Lozada, L. G., Herrera-Acosta, J., & Johnson, R. J. (2006). Uric Acid ⊠ A Uremic Toxin? *Blood Purification, 24*, 67–70. https://doi.org/10.1159/000089440

20. Treviño-Becerra A., & Iseki, K.(2018). Uric Acid: The Unknown Uremic Toxin. Contributions to Nephrology, 192, 25–33. https://doi.org/10.1159/000484275

21. Pascual-Figal, D. A., Hurtado-Martínez, J. A., Redondo, B., Antolinos, M. J., Ruiperez, J. A., & Valdes, M. (2007). Hyperuricaemia and long-term outcome after hospital discharge in acute heart failure patients. *European Journal of Heart Failure, 9*(5), 518–524. https://doi.org/10.1016/j.ejheart.2006.09.001

22. Mazza, A., Zamboni, S., Rizzato, E., Pessina, A. C., Tikhonoff, V., Schiavon, L., & Casiglia, E. (2007). Serum uric acid shows a J-shaped trend with coronary mortality in non-insulin-dependent diabetic elderly people: The Cardiovascular Study in the Elderly (CASTEL). *Acta Diabetologica, 44*(3), 99–105. https://doi.org/10.1007/s00592-007-0249-3

23. Corona, G., Norello, D., Parenti, G., Sforza, A., Maggi, M., & Peri, A. (2018). Hyponatremia, falls and bone fractures: A systematic review and meta-analysis. *Clinical Endocrinology, 89*(4), 505–513. https://doi.org/10.1111/cen.13790

24. Hoorn, E. J., Rivadeneira, F., van Meurs, J. B., Ziere, G., Stricker, B. H., Hofman, A., Pols, H. A., Zietse, R., Uitterlinden, A. G., & Zillikens, M. C. (2011). Mild hyponatremia as a risk factor for fractures: the Rotterdam Study. *Journal of Bone and Mineral Research, 26*(8), 1822–1828. https://doi.org/10.1002/jbmr.380

25. Rodrigues, B., Staff, I., Fortunato, G., & McCullough, L. D. (2014). Hyponatremia in the progno-sis of acute ischemic stroke. *Journal of Stroke and Cerebrovascular Diseases, 23*(5), 850–854. https://doi.org/10.1016/j.jstrokecerebrovasdis.2013.07.011

26. Mansoor, F., Kumar, J., Kaur, N., Sultan, S., Tahir, H., Dilip, A., Khan, F., Kumar, N., Khalid, H., & Talpur, A. S. (2021). Frequency of Electrolyte Imbalance in Patients Presenting With Acute Stroke. *Cureus, 13*(9), e18307. https://doi.org/10.7759/cureus.18307

27. Wannamethee, G., Whincup, P. H., Shaper, A. G., & Lever, A. F. (1994). Serum sodium concentra-tion and risk of stroke in middle-aged males. *Journal of Hypertension, 12*(8), 971–979. https://pubmed.

28. Mansoor, F., Bai, P., Kaur, N., Sultan, S., Sharma, S., Dilip, A., Kammawal, Y., Shahid, S., & Rizwan, A. (2021). Evaluation of Serum Electrolyte Levels in Patients With Anemia. *Cureus, 13*(10), e18417. https://doi.org/10.7759/cureus.18417

29. Wannamethee, S. G., Shaper, A. G., Lennon, L., Papacosta, O., & Whincup, P. (2016). Mild hyponatremia, hypernatremia and incident cardiovascular disease and mortality in older men: A population-based cohort study. *Nutrition, Metabolism, and Cardiovascular Diseases, 26*(1), 12–19. https://doi.org/10.1016/j.numecd.2015.07.008

30. Oh, S. W., Baek, S. H., An, J. N., Goo, H. S., Kim, S., Na, K. Y., Chae, D. W., Kim, S., & Chin, H. J. (2013). Small increases in plasma sodium are associated with higher risk of mortality in a healthy population. *Journal of Korean Medical Science, 28*(7), 1034–1040. https://doi.org/10.3346/jkms.2013.28.7.1034

31. Hughes-Austin, J. M., Rifkin, D. E., Beben, T., Katz, R., Sarnak, M. J., Deo, R., Hoofnagle, A. N., Homma, S., Siscovick, D. S., Sotoodehnia, N., Psaty, B. M., de Boer, I. H., Kestenbaum, B., Shlipak, M. G., & Ix, J. H. (2017). The Relation of Serum Potassium Concentration with Cardiovascular Events and Mortality in Community-Living Individuals. *Clinical Journal of the American Society of Nephrology, 12*(2), 245–252. https://doi.org/10.2215/CJN.06290616

32. Krogager, M. L., Torp-Pedersen, C., Mortensen, R. N., Køber, L., Gislason, G., Søgaard, P., & Aasbjerg, K. (2017). Short-term mortality risk of serum potassium levels in hypertension: a retrospective analysis of nationwide registry data. *European Heart Journal, 38*(2), 104–112. https://doi.org/10.1093/eurheartj/ehw129

33. Ahmed, M. I., Ekundayo, O. J., Mujib, M., Campbell, R. C., Sanders, P. W., Pitt, B., Perry, G. J., Bakris, G., Aban, I., Love, T. E., Aronow, W. S., & Ahmed, A. (2010). Mild hyperkalemia and outcomes in chronic heart failure: a propensity matched study. *International Journal of Cardiology, 144*(3), 383–388. https://doi.org/10.1016/j.ijcard.2009.04.041

34. Collins, A. J., Pitt, B., Reaven, N., Funk, S., McGaughey, K., Wilson, D., & Bushinsky, D. A. (2017). Association of Serum Potassium with All-Cause Mortality in Patients with and without Heart Failure, Chronic Kidney Disease, and/or Diabetes. *American Journal of Nephrology, 46*(3), 213–221. https://doi.

org/10.1159/000479802

35. Fang, J., Madhavan, S., Cohen, H., & Alderman, M. H. (2000). Serum potassium and cardiovascular mortality. *Journal of General Internal Medicine, 15*(12), 885–890. https://doi.org/10.1046/j.1525-1497.2000.91021.x

36. Sica, D. A., Struthers, A. D., Cushman, W. C., Wood, M., Banas, J. S., Jr, & Epstein, M. (2002). Importance of potassium in cardiovascular disease. *Journal of Clinical Hypertension, 4*(3), 198–206. https://doi.org/10.1111/j.1524-6175.2002.01728.x

37. Mattu, A., Brady, W. J., & Robinson, D. A. (2000). Electrocardiographic manifestations of hyperkalemia. *The American Journal of Emergency Medicine, 18*(6), 721–729. https://doi.org/10.1053/ajem.2000.7344

38. Ohmae, M., & Rabkin, S. W. (1981). Hyperkalemia-induced bundle branch block and complete heart block. *Clinical Cardiology, 4*(1), 43–46. https://doi.org/10.1002/clc.4960040110

39. An, J. N., Lee, J. P., Jeon, H. J., Kim, D. H., Oh, Y. K., Kim, Y. S., & Lim, C. S. (2012). Severe hyperkalemia requiring hospitalization: predictors of mortality. *Critical Care, 16*(6), R225. https://doi.org/10.1186/cc11872

40. Ahmed, A., Zannad, F., Love, T. E., Tallaj, J., Gheorghiade, M., Ekundayo, O. J., & Pitt, B. (2007). A propensity-matched study of the association of low serum potassium levels and mortality in chronic heart failure. *European Heart Journal, 28*(11), 1334–1343. https://doi.org/10.1093/eurheartj/ehm091

41. Grobbee, D. E., & Hoes, A. W. (1995). Non-potassium-sparing diuretics and risk of sudden cardiac death. *Journal of Hypertension, 13*(12 Pt 2), 1539–1545. https://pubmed.ncbi.nlm.nih.gov/8903607/

42. Siscovick, D. S., Raghunathan, T. E., Psaty, B. M., Koepsell, T. D., Wicklund, K. G., Lin, X., Cobb, L., Rautaharju, P. M., Copass, M. K., & Wagner, E. H. (1994). Diuretic therapy for hypertension and the risk of primary cardiac arrest. *The New England Journal of Medicine, 330*(26), 1852–1857. https://doi.org/10.1056/NEJM199406303302603

43. Overlack, A., Maus, B., Ruppert, M., Lennarz, M., Kolloch, R., & Stumpe, K. O. (1995). Kaliumcitrat versus Kaliumchlorid bei essentieller Hypertonie. Wirkung auf hämodynamische, hormonelle und

metabolische Parameter [Potassium citrate vs potassium chloride in essential hypertension: Effect on haemodynamic, hormonal and metabolic parameters]. *Deutsche Medizinische Wochenschrift, 120*(18), 631–635. https://doi.org/10.1055/s-2008-1055388

44. Walsh, C. R., Larson, M. G., Leip, E. P., Vasan, R. S., & Levy, D. (2002). Serum Potassium and Risk of Cardiovascular Disease: The Framingham Heart Study. *Archives of Internal Medicine, 162*(9), 1007–1012. https://doi.org/10.1001/archinte.162.9.1007

45. Chen, Y., Chang, A. R., McAdams DeMarco, M. A., Inker, L. A., Matsushita, K., Ballew, S. H., Coresh, J., & Grams, M. E. (2016). Serum Potassium, Mortality, and Kidney Outcomes in the Atherosclerosis Risk in Communities Study. *Mayo Clinic Proceedings, 91*(10), 1403–1412. https://doi.org/10.1016/j.mayocp.2016.05.018

46. Newberry, S. J., Chung, M., Anderson, C. A. M., Chen, C., Fu, Z., Tang, A., Zhao, N., Booth, M., Marks, J., Hollands, S., Motala, A., Larkin, J. K., Shanman, R. and Hempel, S. (2018) *Sodium and Potassium Intake: Effects on Chronic Disease Outcomes and Risks (Comparative Effectiveness Review, No. 206)*. Agency for Healthcare Research and Quality. https://www.ncbi.nlm.nih.gov/books/NBK519328/

47. Krijthe, B. P., Heeringa, J., Kors, J. A., Hofman, A., Franco, O. H., Witteman, J. C., & Stricker, B. H. (2013). Serum potassium levels and the risk of atrial fibrillation: The Rotterdam Study. *International Journal of Cardiology, 168*(6), 5411–5415. https://doi.org/10.1016/j.ijcard.2013.08.048

48. Goyal, A., Spertus, J. A., Gosch, K., Venkitachalam, L., Jones, P. G., Van den Berghe, G., & Kosiborod, M. (2012). Serum potassium levels and mortality in acute myocardial infarction. *JAMA, 307*(2), 157–164. https://doi.org/10.1001/jama.2011.1967

49. Royal Society of Chemistry (n.d.) *Periodic Table: Chlorine*. Retrieved October 31, 2022, from https://www.rsc.org/periodic-table/element/17/chlorine

50. De Bacquer, D., De Backer, G., De Buyzere, M., & Kornitzer, M. (1998). Is low serum chloride level a risk factor for cardiovascular mortality? *Journal of Cardiovascular Risk, 5*(3), 177–184. https://doi.org/10.1186/s40635-018-0174-5

51. McCallum, L., Jeemon, P., Hastie, C. E., Patel, R. K., Williamson, C., Redzuan, A. M., Dawson, J.,

Sloan, W., Muir, S., Morrison, D., McInnes, G. T., Freel, E. M., Walters, M., Dominiczak, A. F., Sattar, N., & Padmanabhan, S. (2013). Serum chloride is an independent predictor of mortality in hypertensive patients. *Hypertension, 62*(5), 836–843. https://doi.org/10.1161/HYPERTENSIONAHA.113.01793

52. Mandel, E. I., Curhan, G. C., Hu, F. B., & Taylor, E. N. (2012). Plasma bicarbonate and risk of type 2 diabetes mellitus. *Canadian Medical Association Journal, 184*(13), E719–E725. https://doi.org/10.1503/cmaj.120438

53. Abramowitz, M. K., Hostetter, T. H., & Melamed, M. L. (2012). Lower serum bicarbonate and a higher anion gap are associated with lower cardiorespiratory fitness in young adults. *Kidney International, 81*(10), 1033–1042. https://doi.org/10.1038/ki.2011.479

54. Farwell, W. R., & Taylor, E. N. (2010). Serum anion gap, bicarbonate and biomarkers of inflammation in healthy individuals in a national survey. *Canadian Medical Association Journal, 182*(2), 137–141. https://doi.org/10.1503/cmaj.090329

55. Raphael, K. L., Murphy, R. A., Shlipak, M. G., Satterfield, S., Huston, H. K., Sebastian, A., Sellmeyer, D. E., Patel, K. V., Newman, A. B., Sarnak, M. J., Ix, J. H., & Fried, L. F. Fir the Health ABC Study. (2016). Bicarbonate Concentration, Acid-Base Status, and Mortality in the Health, Aging, and Body Composition Study. *Clinical Journal of the American Society of Nephrology,* 11(2), 308–316. https://doi.org/10.2215/CJN.06200615

56. Driver, T. H., Shlipak, M. G., Katz, R., Goldenstein, L., Sarnak, M. J., Hoofnagle, A. N., Siscovick, D. S., Kestenbaum, B., de Boer, I. H., & Ix, J. H. (2014). Low serum bicarbonate and kidney function decline: the Multi-Ethnic Study of Atherosclerosis (MESA). *American Journal of Kidney Diseases, 64*(4), 534–541. https://doi.org/10.1053/j.ajkd.2014.05.008

57. Abramowitz, M. K., Hostetter, T. H., & Melamed, M. L. (2011). Association of serum bicarbonate levels with gait speed and quadriceps strength in older adults. *American Journal of Kidney Diseases, 58*(1), 29–38. https://doi.org/10.1053/j.ajkd.2010.12.021

58. Leifsson, B. G., & Ahrén, B. (1996). Serum calcium and survival in a large health screening program. *The Journal of Clinical Endocrinology & Metabolism, 81*(6), 2149–2153. https://doi.org/10.1210/jcem.81.6.8964843

59. Guessous, I., Bonny, O., Paccaud, F., Mooser, V., Waeber, G., Vollenweider, P., & Bochud, M. (2011). Serum calcium levels are associated with novel cardiometabolic risk factors in the population-based CoLaus study. *PLOS ONE, 6*(4), e18865. https://doi.org/10.1371/journal.pone.0018865

60. Saltevo, J., Niskanen, L., Kautiainen, H., Teittinen, J., Oksa, H., Korpi-Hyövälti, E., Sundvall, J., Männistö, S., Peltonen, M., Mäntyselkä, P., & Vanhala, M. (2011). Serum calcium level is associated with metabolic syndrome in the general population: FIN-D2D study. *European Journal of Endocrinology, 165*(3), 429–434. https://doi.org/10.1530/EJE-11-0066

61. Hagström, E., Hellman, P., Lundgren, E., Lind, L., & Ärnlöv, J. (2007). Serum calcium is independently associated with insulin sensitivity measured with euglycaemic-hyperinsulinaemic clamp in a community-based cohort. *Diabetologia, 50*(2), 317–324. https://doi.org/10.1007/s00125-006-0532-9

62. Harper, D. (n.d.). Etymology of albumin. In *Online Etymology Dictionary*. Retrieved October 31, 2022, from https://www.etymonline.com/word/albumin

63. Seidu, S., Kunutsor, S. K., & Khunti, K. (2020). Serum albumin, cardiometabolic and other adverse outcomes: systematic review and meta-analyses of 48 published observational cohort studies involving 1,492,237 participants. *Scandinavian Cardiovascular Journal, 54*(5), 280–293. https://doi.org/10.1080/14017431.2020.1762918

64. Kadono, M., Hasegawa, G., Shigeta, M., Nakazawa, A., Ueda, M., Yamazaki, M., Fukui, M., & Nakamura, N. (2010). Serum albumin levels predict vascular dysfunction with paradoxical pathogenesis in healthy individuals. *Atherosclerosis, 209*(1), 266–270. https://doi.org/10.1016/j.atherosclerosis.2009.09.006

65. Harper, D. (n.d.). Etymology of globule. In *Online Etymology Dictionary*. Retrieved October 31, 2022, from https://www.etymonline.com/word/globule

66. Berger M. (2002). A history of immune globulin therapy, from the Harvard crash program to monoclonal antibodies. *Current Allergy and Asthma Reports, 2*(5), 368–378. https://doi.org/10.1007/s11882-002-0069-z

67. Pai, A. Y., Sy, J., Kim, J., Kleine, C. E., Edward, J., Hsiung, J. T., Kovesdy, C. P., Kalantar-Zadeh,

K., & Streja, E. (2022). Association of serum globulin with all-cause mortality in incident hemodialysis patients. *Nephrology Dialysis Transplantation, 37*(10), 1993–2003. https://doi.org/10.1093/ndt/gfab292

68. American Chemical Society. (2017, March 27) *Molecule of the Week Archive: Bilirubin.* https://www.acs.org/molecule-of-the-week/archive/b/bilirubin.html

69. Fulks, M., Stout, R. L., & Dolan, V. F. (2009). Mortality associated with bilirubin levels in insurance applicants. *Journal of Insurance Medicine, 41*(1), 49–53. https://www.ncbi.nlm.nih.gov/pubmed/19518005

70. Karuppannasamy, D., Venkatesan, R., Thankappan, L., Andavar, R., & Devisundaram, S. (2017). Inverse Association between Serum Bilirubin Levels and Retinopathy in Patients with Type 2 Diabetes Mellitus. *Journal of Clinical and Diagnostic Research, 11*(2), NC09–NC12. https://doi.org/10.7860/JCDR/2017/24259.9452

71. Baran Barañano, D. E., Rao, M., Ferris, C. D., & Snyder, S. H. (2002). Biliverdin reductase: A major physiologic cytoprotectant. *Proceedings of the National Academy of Sciences of the United States of America, 99*(25), 16093–16098. https://doi.org/10.1073/pnas.252626999

72. Fulks, M., Stout, R. L., & Dolan, V. F. (2009). Mortality associated with bilirubin levels in insurance applicants. *Journal of Insurance Medicine, 41*(1), 49–53. https://www.ncbi.nlm.nih.gov/pubmed/19518005

73. Tatami, Y., Suzuki, S., Ishii, H., Shibata, Y., Osugi, N., Ota, T., Kawamura, Y., Tanaka, A., Takeshita, K., & Murohara, T. (2014). Impact of serum bilirubin levels on carotid atherosclerosis in patients with coronary artery disease, *IJC Metabolic & Endocrine, 5*, 24–27. https://doi.org/10.1016/j.ijcme.2014.08.006

74. Zhang, Z. Y., Bian, L. Q., Jae, S. Y., Sung, J. D., & Choi, Y. H. (2013). Serum total bilirubin is inversely associated with brachial-ankle pulse wave velocity in men with hypertension. *Heart and Vessels, 28*, 453–460. https://doi.org/10.1007/s00380-012-0261-6

75. Chen, Z., He, J., Chen, C., & Lu, Q. (2021). Association of Total Bilirubin With All-Cause and Cardiovascular Mortality in the General Population. *Frontiers in Cardiovascular Medicine, 18*(6), 721–729. https://doi.org/10.3389/fcvm.2021.670768

76. Siller, A. F., & Whyte, M. P. (2018). Alkaline Phosphatase: Discovery and Naming of Our Favorite Enzyme. *Journal of Bone and Mineral Research, 33*(2), 362–364. https://doi.org/10.1002/jbmr.3225

77. Lowe D., Sanvictores T., Zubair M., & Savio, J. *Alkaline Phosphatase* (updated ed.). StatPearls Publishing. https://www.ncbi.nlm.nih.gov/books/NBK459201/

78. Hu, G., & Duncan, A. W. (2013). Associations between selected laboratory tests and all-cause mortality. *Journal of Insurance Medicine, 43*(4), 208–220. https://www.ncbi.nlm.nih.gov/pubmed/24069781

79. Hyeon, C. K., Chung, M. N., Sun, H.J., Kwang, H. H., Oh, D. K., & Suh, I. (2004). Normal serum aminotransferase concentration and risk of mortality from liver diseases: prospective cohort study. *BMJ,* 328, 983. https://doi.org/10.1136/bmj.38050.593634.63

80. Ndrepepa, G., Holdenrieder, S., Cassese, S., Xhepa, E., Fusaro, M., Laugwitz, K. L., Schunkert, H., & Kastrati, A. (2020). Aspartate aminotransferase and mortality in patients with ischemic heart disease. *Nutrition, Metabolism, and Cardiovascular Diseases, 30*(12), 2335–2342. https://doi.org/10.1016/j.numecd.2020.07.033

81. Wu, W. C., Wu, C. Y., Wang, Y. J., Hung, H. H., Yang, H. I., Kao, W. Y., Su, C. W., Wu, J. C., Chan, W. L., Lin, H. C., Lee, F. Y., & Lee, S. D. (2012). Updated thresholds for serum alanine aminotransferase level in a large-scale population study composed of 34 346 subjects. *Alimentary Pharmacology and Therapeutics, 36*(6), 560–568. https://doi.org/10.1111/j.1365-2036.2012.05224.x

82. Kang, H. S., Um, S. H., Seo, Y. S., An, H., Lee, K. G., Hyun, J. J., Kim, E. S., Park, S. C., Keum, B., Kim, J. H., Yim, H. J., Jeen, Y. T., Lee, H. S., Chun, H. J., Kim, C. D., & Ryu, H. S. (2010). Healthy range for serum ALT and the clinical significance of "unhealthy" normal ALT levels in the Korean population. *Journal of Gastroenterology and Hepatology, 26*(2), 292–299. https://doi.org/10.1111/j.1440-1746.2010.06481.x

83. Yuen, M. F., Yuan, H. J., Wong, D. K., Yuen, J. C., Wong, W. M., Chan, A. O., Wong, B. C., Lai, K. C., & Lai, C. L. (2005). Prognostic determinants for chronic hepatitis B in Asians: therapeutic implications. *Gut, 54*(11), 1610–1614. https://doi.org/10.1136/gut.2005.065136

84. Kumada, T., Toyoda, H., Kiriyama, S., Sone, Y., Tanikawa, M., Hisanaga, Y., Kanamori, A., Atsumi,

H., Takagi, M., Nakano, S., Arakawa, T., & Fujimori, M. (2009). Incidence of hepatocellular carcinoma in hepatitis C carriers with normal alanine aminotransferase levels. *Journal of Hepatology, 50*(4), 729–735. https://doi.org/10.1016/j.jhep.2008.11.019

85. Degertekin B., Tozun N., Demir F., Soylemez G., Yapali S., Bozkurt U., Gurtay E., Seymenoglu T. H., Mutlu D., & Toraman M. (2020) Determination of the upper limits of normal serum alanine aminotransferase (ALT) level in healthy Turkish population. *Hepatol Forum, 1*(2) 44–47. https://doi.org/10.14744/hf.2020.2020.0012

86. Hyeon, C. K., Chung, M. N., Sun, H.J., Kwang, H. H., Oh, D. K., & Suh, I. (2004). Normal serum aminotransferase concentration and risk of mortality from liver diseases: prospective cohort study. *BMJ, 328*, 983. https://doi.org/10.1136/bmj.38050.593634.63

87. Kabir, A., Pourshams, A., Khoshnia, M., & Malekzadeh, F. (2013). Normal limit for serum alanine aminotransferase level and distribution of metabolic factors in old population of Kalaleh, Iran. *Hepatitis Monthly, 13*(10), e10640. https://doi.org/10.5812/hepatmon.10640

88. Ndrepepa, G., Holdenrieder, S., Colleran, R., Cassese, S., Xhepa, E., Fusaro, M., Laugwitz, K. L., Schunkert, H., & Kastrati, A. (2019). Inverse association of alanine aminotransferase within normal range with prognosis in patients with coronary artery disease. *Clinica Chimica Acta: International Journal of Clinical Chemistry and Diagnostic Laboratory Medicine, 496*, 55–61. https://doi.org/10.1016/j.cca.2019.06.021

89. Siddiqui, M. S., Sterling, R. K., Luketic, V. A., Puri, P., Stravitz, R. T., Bouneva, I., Boyett, S., Fuchs, M., Sargeant, C., Warnick, G. R., Grami, S., & Sanyal, A. J. (2013). Association between high-normal levels of alanine aminotransferase and risk factors for atherogenesis. *Gastroenterology, 145*(6), 1271–1279. https://doi.org/10.1053/j.gastro.2013.08.036

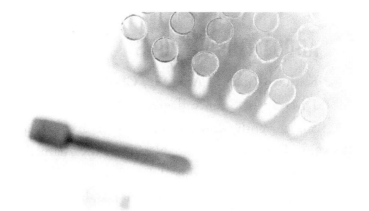

ACKNOWLEDGMENTS

Everything I know, I learned from my patients.

ABOUT THE AUTHORS

Kathryn Black, LAc, MSc, CFMP, is a licensed acupuncturist with a Master of Science degree and is certified in functional medicine. She currently works as an acupuncturist and patient care coordinator alongside Dr. John Nieters at the Alameda Acupuncture Clinic in Alameda, California. USA. She specializes in combining Chinese medicine with the usage and insights of functional medicine lab values. She also specializes in inflammatory bowel disease and other digestive ailments.

Kathryn received her certificate in functional medicine from Functional Medicine University. She received her bachelor's degree in music therapy from Arizona State University and has practiced in a variety of settings including Muhammad Ali Parkinson Clinic, Utah State Developmental Center, Alcoholics Anonymous, and has worked with children with developmental disabilities and in hospice. She started the music therapy program at Utah State Hospital. She presented several years on music therapy and addiction at Utah's Substance Abuse Conference.

Kathryn's favorite activity is spending time with her dog Opie.

Dr. John R. Nieters, LAc, DAOM, DNBAO, MSc, CFMP, NCCAOM, has earned certificates in gynecology from Zhejiang University, China, and integrative diabetes care from Xin Hua hospital, Hongzhou, China.

Dr. John began his studies in Chinese medicine with Master Y.C. Chiang in Berkeley, California, studying Tai Ji Chuan and Qi Gong as well as being introduced to herbal studies. He continued his martial arts and contemplative studies as a master apprentice trainer at the Cheng Hsin School of Internal Martial Arts and Ontological Studies with 1978 World Martial Arts champion, Peter Ralston. John was given a full teaching license to teach the Cheng Hsin arts in 1992.

John received his Master of Science degree from the Academy of Chinese Culture and Health Sciences, ACCHS. He began teaching at ACCHS in 1998.

Shortly after his graduation from ACCHS, John finished his advanced orthopedics training and received the title of Diplomate National Board of Acupuncture Orthopedics (DNBAO).

John received his doctorate from Five Branches University in San Jose, California. His area of specialization was gynecological endocrinology. John also did PhD work on breast health at Zhejiang University, China.

In his free time, John loves spending time with his wife, Jenny, and his loving children, Nick, Katelynn, and Johnny.

INDEX

A

alkaline phosphatase   23, 24, 25, 47, 98, 99, 100

all-cause mortality   50, 88

ALP   *See* Alkaline phosphatase

ALT   5, 101, 102, 105, 106, 107, 108, 109, 110, 111, 112, 113, 114

amino acid   75, 105

ammonia   22, 105

ampullary adenocarcinoma   99

anemia 45, 46, 87, 91, 100

anion gap   69, 70, 71

antibiotics   49

antibody deficiencies   87, 89

antifungals   49

antioxidant   83, 85, 94, 113

arrhythmia   61, 77

arrhythmias   51, 61, 62

arterial stiffness 20, 96, 121

Arterial stiffness   91, 97

Arterial Stiffness   20

arthritis   36

aspartate aminotransferase   *See* AST

Aspartate aminotransferase   *See* AST

Aspartate transferase   *See* AST

AST   4, 5, 101, 102, 103, 104, 105, 106, 109, 110

asystole 51

chronic infections   87, 89

chronic kidney disease 29, 30, 31, 32, 35, 38, 50, 54, 57, 62, 70, 72, 73, 93, 121, *See* CKD

chronic obstructive pulmonary disease *See* COPD

cirrhosis   107, 108

cirrhosis of the liver   108

CKD   29, 31, 35, 38, 54

CO_2 3, 67, 68, 70, 71, 72

cognitive problems   41, 47

community-based population 59

Complete Heart Block 56

Confusion   77

Constipation   76

COPD 68

copper 100

coronary artery disease 91, 93, 95, 113

corticosteroids 49

cortisol 42

C-reactive protein   70, 71

creatinine   26, 27, 28, 29, 30, 31, 71, 121

Cushing's syndrome   49

CVD   *See* Cardiovascular Disease

cysts   36

D

death   13, 16, 17, 18, 20, 37, 38, 43, 51, 52, 53, 60, 64, 71, 78, 84,

91, 121

diabetes, 91, 121 — continued

dehydrated	22

dehydration	14, 83

Dehydration	23, 35, 64, 68

Depression	77

DEXA scan	76

diabetes	8, 12, 14, 17, 18, 19, 21, 31, 33, 37, 50, 54, 57, 68, 69, 70, 73, 79, 80, 84, 91, 92, 93, 117, 121

Diabetes	12, 13, 19, 49, 54, 69, 92, 121

diabetes mellitus	13, 31, 32, 50, 54, 69

diabetes risk	69, 80, 91, 96, 97

diabetic peripheral neuropathy 93

diabetic retinopathy	92, 93

diabetic risk	18

diarrhea	49

Diarrhea	64

diastolic	21, 47, 57, 59

Diastolic	57

diet	8, 14, 29, 31, 49

digestive	8, 63, 90, 111, 112, 117

digestive diseases	111

diuretic58

Diuretic	51, 58, 68

diuretics	49, 50, 51, 52, 57, 58, 60

dizziness	41, 43, 47

intracellular fluid   48

iron   24, 46, 74

Irritability   77

Ischemic   45, 103

J

J-shaped   11, 15, 17, 20, 23, 25, 38, 94

K

ketoacidosis   68

Ketogenic diet 35

kidney 15, 22, 30, 32, 36, 49, 54, 55, 57, 67, 68, 70, 71, 72, 80, 105, 121

kidney damage 31

kidney disease 30, 31, 32, 33, 37, 49, 62, 70, 72, 83, 87, 89, 91

Kidney disease 35, 64, 76, 87, 97

kidney diseases 27, 36

kidney failure 22, 31, 57

kidney function   22, 26, 30, 31, 37, 57, 68, 70, 72

kidney functions   26

kidney outcomes   60

kidney pathologies   102

kidney stones 32, 34

kidneys 13, 22, 23, 25, 26, 27, 28, 29, 30, 31, 32, 35, 38, 39, 43, 48, 61, 63, 75, 76, 82

L

lactate dehydrogenase 25

Made in the USA
Middletown, DE
13 August 2024